Building Bridges
With Parents

Practical Skills for Counselors
Jeffrey A. Kottler, Series Editor

Building Bridges With Parents: Tools and Techniques for Counselors
Marilyn J. Montgomery

Assisting Students With Disabilities: What School Counselors Can and Must Do
Julie P. Baumberger, Ruth E. Harper

All About Sex: The School Counselor's Guide to Handling Tough Adolescent Problems
Loretta J. Bradley, Elaine Jarchow, Beth Robinson

Narrative Counseling in Schools: Powerful & Brief
John Winslade, Gerald Monk

Helping in the Hallways: Advanced Strategies for Enhancing School Relationships
Richard J. Hazler

Brief Counseling That Works: A Solution-Focused Approach for School Counselors
Gerald B. Sklare

Deciphering the Diagnostic Codes: A Guide for School Counselors
W. Paul Jones

Success With Challenging Students
Jeffrey A. Kottler

Marilyn J. Montgomery

Building Bridges With Parents

Tools and Techniques for Counselors

CORWIN PRESS, INC.
A Sage Publications Company
Thousand Oaks, California

For information:

Corwin Press, Inc.
A Sage Publications Company
2455 Teller Road
Thousand Oaks, California 91320
E-mail: order@corwinpress.com

SAGE Publications Ltd.
6 Bonhill Street
London EC2A 4PU
United Kingdom

SAGE Publications India Pvt. Ltd.
M-32 Market
Greater Kailash I
New Delhi 110 048 India

Printed in the United States of America

Library of Congress Cataloging-in-Publication Data

Montgomery, Marilyn J.
  Building bridges with parents: Tools and techniques for counselors / by Marilyn J. Montgomery.
    p. cm. — (Practical skills for counselors)
  Includes bibliographical references and index.
  ISBN 0-8039-6708-X (cloth: acid-free paper)
  ISBN 0-8039-6709-8 (pbk.: acid-free paper)
  1. Educational counseling. 2. Parent-student counselor relationships. 3. Parenting. I. Title. II. Series.
  LB1027.5 .M564 1999
  371.4'2—dc21   98-40273

This book is printed on acid-free paper.

99 00 01 02 03 10 9 8 7 6 5 4 3 2 1

Editorial Assistant: Kristen L. Gibson
Production Editor: Diana E. Axelsen
Editorial Assistant: Patricia Zeman
Typesetter/Designer: Danielle Dillahunt
Cover Designer: Michelle Lee

Contents

Preface   **vii**
  Contents of the Book   viii
  Acknowledgements   ix

About the Author   **x**

1. Why Deal With Parents?   **1**
  Why Bother?   3
  Parents as Developing People   5
  Creating a Vision for Parent Participation   9

2. Tools and Techniques for Building Bridges   **14**
  Planning the Bridge: What Is the Goal?   17
  Clearing and Leveling the Ground:
    Removing Barriers   19
  Building the Bridge: Gaining Cooperation   24
  Using and Maintaining the Bridge: Parent Contacts,
    Conferences, and Consultations   28

3. Troubled Kids, Anxious Parents   **32**
  Parents' Themes of Anxiety   34
  Countering Anxious Themes   38
  Extended Family Members Raising Kids   44

4. **Inviting Parents to Become Involved**   **46**
   Developing a Comprehensive
      Home-School Partnership   48
   Promoting Student Academic Success   51
   Promoting Student Vocational Success   52
   Promoting Parenting Skills
      and Family Emotional Health   54
   Promoting Parent Development
      and Family Empowerment   59

5. **Tips From the Trenches:**
   Creating Successful Programs for Parents   **66**
   Know Your Parents   67
   Consider Your Community   67
   Plan Your Program   68
   Be a Charismatic Leader   70
   Motivate and Encourage   71
   Have a Great First Meeting   73
   Emphasize Active Learning   74
   Aim for Good Closure   75

**Resource A: Resources for Building
Parent Participation**   **77**

Resource B: Suggested Readings   **79**

References   **81**

Index   **83**

Preface

School counselors do not work alone. After 1 week on the job, any school counselor's vision of a quiet life of heart-to-heart chats with troubled students has shrunk to make room for the overwhelming number of other responsibilities that are part of the job. In addition to intervening with students and tracking paperwork, the school counselor is expected to interact with every student, teacher, administrator, and parent in a supportive way that facilitates cooperative involvement. In fact, the American School Counseling Association defines the school counselor as a *collaborator* who facilitates communication and establishes linkages for the benefit of students by consulting with teachers, administrators, and parents to assist students to be successful academically, vocationally, and personally. This bridge-building work is an essential part of being a school counselor.

Of all the people counselors must interface with to help aim students toward success, parents are the hardest to reach. Although teachers and administrators may not always agree with guidance plans or intervention strategies, they are at least available on-site for negotiation. Parents, on the other hand, are often difficult to locate and even more challenging to involve. (And then there are the parents whom we wish were a little *less* involved!) How can school counselors build bridges to students' parents or guardians? What do school counselors have to offer parents that will help each student be successful—academically, vocationally, and personally? What kinds of programs and techniques are really effective in reaching parents? How can school counselors deal with parents who are overconcerned and underinvolved or whose decisions make no sense to us? How can we find the time to keep in touch with parents when so many other responsibilities call our name?

Contents of the Book

This book will confirm for you the importance of efforts to involve parents. Chapter 1 provides facts counselors can use to persuade other school personnel of the importance of investing in parent outreach efforts. Chapter 2 provides practical suggestions for initiating contacts with parents or guardians and facilitating smooth interactions with them. In Chapter 3, a framework for understanding different types of anxious parents is introduced, along with techniques for working with these types of families. In Chapter 4, you will find an overview of various programs other school counselors have found useful and effective for attaining various outcomes such as parent education, academic support at home, therapeutic support at home, and involvement of at-risk families. Chapter 5 concludes the book with a collection of tried-and-true techniques counselors have used to create successful experiences with parents.

I wish to mention up front that although this book is titled *Building Bridges With Parents*, I know that there are many men and women in our communities who take on the heroic task of raising a child who is not biologically their own—they are providing "parenting," though they may not actually be the child's parents. These adults are sometimes called *caregivers*, and that word does indeed capture the nurturing and the generosity involved in their task. In this book, I sometimes specifically address nonparental caregivers (in Chapter 3, for example), but most of the time, when I use the word *parents,* I mean these other brave adults as well.

Acknowledgments

I remember with gratitude the many children and families I have known through my years in the schools and as a counselor. Patiently, families in East Texas, the Rio Grande Valley, and several West Texas and Texas Panhandle towns suffered through my misplaced idealism, my discouragement, and my misunderstandings and eventually taught me that compassion, curiosity, and constructiveness are the best tools of a bridge builder. These are the first tools I unpacked when I relocated in South Florida. I am still a stranger to many ways of life here, but I know these tools will serve me well as I get to know families here.

I also reflect with gratitude on the years I spent working with students in the school counseling program at Texas Tech University, where I was until recently a faculty member in counselor education. We talked through cases together, interfaced with schools, leaned on school counseling veterans for guidance with ticklish situations, and sought out state and local school counseling directors to discuss the heavy (and impossibly demanding) responsibilities resulting from a counselor's multiple roles. Some of these stories are included in this book, but names and identifying circumstances have been changed to protect the confidentiality of all involved.

Nevertheless, these are stories of courageous and creative counselors whose compassionate work, most fortunately, goes on. To them, I dedicate this book.

About the Author

Marilyn J. Montgomery is Assistant Professor of Psychology at Florida International University, where she specializes in enhancing relationships between parents and children. She began her career teaching at-risk students in middle and secondary vocational schools. She was later the director of the Child Development Research Center at Texas Tech University and founder of the Wellspring Center for Child and Family Development. Working with the families of her students as a teacher, an administrator, and a counselor developed her interest in building bridges with parents. She continues to consult with several state and local agencies on family and educational issues. She is also the author of *1, 2, 3, 4 Parents* (with Michael Popkin and Betsy Gard, Active Parenting Publishers, 1996).

1

Why Deal With Parents?

The counseling profession has long recognized that the school environment is only one dimension of a child's life. Home and community both greatly affect a student's resources for success, perhaps even more so than school. Although counselors are responsible for providing direct service to students, they are also charged with providing system support to the staff of the school and to parents and guardians of students. So, rather than providing a quiet refuge for troubled students in a small office away from the fray, school counselors are now expected to do whatever it takes to prevent as well as ameliorate problems. And that means acting as a broker of wisdom and goodwill to the families from which students come and a mediator between these families and the (often baffling) school system to which they send their children for an education.

More and more often, school districts are insisting that school counselors provide services to parents and guardians as well as children. In Dade County, Florida, for example, a statement of parent/ guardian rights states specifically that parents or guardians have the right to request special group sessions on educational and career planning; emotional, personal, and social growth; and test-taking skills and interpretation. Parents are also told that they have the right to request information on how to help them communicate with their children and understand their behavior and on programs to help students develop positive self-concepts.

School counselors often feel ill prepared for reaching out to parents and guardians, however. The graduate courses most of us encountered gave a nod to the importance of parental involvement, but didn't supply practical information we could use to reach parents or sustain their interest. Our training programs typically didn't include a chance to practice interventions with families of troubled children that make both the school and the home environment more therapeutic for the child. Once we begin working in the schools, we have few chances to talk with those in the field to find out what, on a practical level, actually works. So we counselors are left with the impression that we should find a way to interact more with families and develop more programs that will help parents help their children more effectively, but we feel overwhelmed about finding time to sort out the options for doing so.

Some of us have put together plans and upbeat, informative programs but have been disappointed about the lack of interest parents seem to have for attending these. We are puzzled about how to reach families in ways that get and keep their attention. Our discouraging experiences have led us to conclude that parents don't care or are so dysfunctional that they can't help. Eventually, some of us feel hopeless or even cynical about having any real beneficial influence on students' families.

The purpose of this book is to address both of these concerns: the "What should I do?" question and the "Why should I keep trying?" question. In the subsequent chapters, I share many stories and practical ideas that school counselors have found effective and helpful in their efforts to intervene constructively with the families of students.

Perhaps some of these will give you ideas for tactics to try in your own locale. But your own efforts will be sustained only when you are convinced—completely convinced—that the things you do to intervene with parents do make a difference—perhaps, sometimes, the biggest and most long-lasting difference you can make. So that is where we begin.

[handwritten marginal note: parents respond to people who are professionals, who are better when they are treated with respect, knowledge of their child.]

Why Bother?

Rather than being a luxury item or a task left for the elusive "someday, when I have time" category, connecting parents with schools is a "must" for counselors who are true advocates of children. Why? Study after study shows that when parents and schools cooperate, there are numerous benefits to children. Even when parents are involved in relatively simple ways, such as occasionally coming into the school and observing what's going on, talking now and then with teachers and counselors, attending programs, or volunteering to help out when possible, children benefit. For example, studies have found the following:

- Children whose parents are involved in their formal education have greater academic achievement.
- Children's motivation for school increases when parents are involved.
- Students' positive attitudes about self and sense of control over their environment are greatly enhanced by parental school involvement.
- Parents' self-concept becomes more positive when they are involved.
- Children from minority and low-income families benefit the most from parental involvement.
- Well-planned and comprehensive parent involvement programs have lasting effects.

What is going on here? Why are these consistently positive results seen when counselors, teachers, and administrators find ways to team up with parents? Apparently, children see parent involvement as a sign that their parents value education—and that they value them. When parents are involved in schools, even in small ways, children recognize that their parents aren't dropping them off and forgetting about them at a free day care service. Instead, involved parents communicate the message that education is an important opportunity for the whole family—a chance for everyone to learn valuable things. When parents are a visible presence in a school, teachers and administrators know that their daily efforts and decisions are important to another group of concerned adults, and this visibility encourages those of us in the schools to "be all that we can be" as professionals. In other words, parents and school professionals can help each reinforce each other's best efforts on behalf of children and help us all remember that what we do every day *matters*.

When counselors find ways to spend more time with parents, offering parents opportunities to find ways to be all that they can be as parents, they are, in effect, providing family interventions and extending their therapeutic skills to influence the larger community. For example, when counselors reach out to parents, parents have an opportunity to observe the counselor's way of thinking about their child's growth and development. Some parents will adapt their discipline patterns (which may be overly permissive or punitive) when they see other techniques that work better with their child modeled by the counselor. Further, when counselors team up with parents, and parents feel increasingly effective with their own child, the parents have a chance to repair poor self-esteem or a diminished sense of competence that may be left over from their own childhood. From experience, we know that parents who feel a greater sense of self-esteem and self-efficacy are more likely to interact with their children in healthy, supportive ways.

Counselors also know the importance of community building among the adults whose children they see every day. Parents can benefit greatly from developing relationships with other parents, and these benefits can be tangible, practical, and emotional. Sociologists have emphasized for years that families with social support are less

Handwritten margin notes:
- Also that the parent really care about what they do?
- Also that it is that a part of Life + Living
- Also what is implemented is school Can be implemented at home? Vise vera
- whear all professi[onal]
- This is why parent groups are so important

likely to develop severely dysfunctional patterns or to abuse their children. Social support simply means knowing others who help out, even in little ways, and having the sense that others care. Parents whose children go to the same school are natural allies. Parents can find comfort in talking to other parents and finding out that they are worried about the same things, going through the same challenges with their own kids, and hoping for the same things for their futures. They can also help each other out with rides to school, looking after each other's kids in the neighborhood, and fostering constructive friendships. Although simple and commonsense at first glance, these things matter a great deal to the well-being of children, who seem to respond positively when a number of adults in their neighborhood form a concerned safety net that never lets them drop beyond reach.

[margin note: This is very important in dealing with the family]

[margin note: This is why parent groups are so important]

The observant counselor sees many of these relationships occurring naturally among parents who are inclined to get involved at school. The flurry of activity around back-to-school night . . . the PTA fund-raising drives . . . the faithful parents who attend the holiday concerts or the band boosters meetings. But what about the ones who seldom darken the door of school . . . for whom no program seems enticing enough, no plea to become involved compelling enough? Is there something to do with these parents besides write them off? One way to prevent the bitterness that sometimes rises within us toward these adults is to remember that when people get the sense that a particular action will actually move them toward something they truly want, then they are likely to take that action. Looking at the problem this way, we see these parents' absence not as a sign of unconcern but as a sign of some aspect of their life experience that we don't understand well enough to connect with . . . yet!

[margin note: Until other people (professionals) connect then they are not successful with parents]

Parents as Developing People

Many experts believe that children are coming to school needier and needier, because the supports that used to exist for children—extended family, community neighborhoods, church-based social networks, and the like—have become less prevalent. Instead of complaining about this and idealizing bygone days, we who care for children have been forced to realize that we must simply take children as they come. *This means taking their parents as they come, too.*

How do they come? Maslow's (1970) hierarchy of needs provides one way to pinpoint the most urgent aspects of life for the parents you hope to reach. Are they struggling with the most basic needs of life—food, clothing, shelter? Or are they trying to feel secure and safe, worried about keeping their children out of danger? A program must "meet parents where they are," and a program targeted at helping parents with the "higher" need to realize their personal potential will be a dismal failure if safety is parents' biggest issue. Likewise, if parents' desire in coming together at the school is to fulfill their needs for affiliation, belonging, and acceptance, the counselor must find a way to acknowledge those needs and meet them within the program, even though there may be other goals (such as providing information) as well.

This lesson came home to me in a way I'll never forget early in my first year of working in schools. I optimistically sent home back-to-school night invitations and prepared eagerly to meet the parents of our challenging middle school charges. The teachers smirked; the principal made snide comments that "No one ever comes anyway, but we have to show up and say we did it." As it turned out, he was almost right. Only a handful of parents came.

I heard many stories in the teachers' lounge about these mysterious, absent parents. How they lived in the local bars; how they got drunk and drove their pickups into the bayous and waved pistols and abused their kids. My job required me to make a certain number of home visits, and naturally, with this kind of introduction, the thought terrified me! But soon after the back-to-school night flop, I summoned up my courage and found my way through the backwoods to see my first parent. Imagine my surprise when I found her walking up from the river in which she had just finished washing her basket full of clothes, extending her hand to me in welcome. Instantly, I realized that reaching out to these parents was going to be very different matter than having attractive bulletin boards or informative handouts. These families were dealing with life issues that had to do with the basics of getting along in the world, not personal growth for themselves or their children. As long as I expected them to act like

(Handwritten margin notes:)
If you can't meet parents where they are, then you aren't doing your job?

Always provide families with information, back it up with written info if possible.

Why do professionals assume parents are no good? If they're not involved with the child, real reason are parents aren't people, not the problem. Putting them down as parents.

people they were not, we would be going nowhere! When I shifted my thinking and talking around to how our school programs were looking for ways to foster skills in students that they could use *now*, in ways that could help out the whole family, these parents responded with more interest.

Another way to gain perspective on parents is to think of them in terms of Erik Erikson's (1963) eight stages of life-span psychosocial development. In many states, this theory of human development is the foundation for the assessments required when determinations must be made about the psychological health of a child or caregiver. Although these stages are related to a person's physical age, they highlight the emotional issues that each of us resolves, to a greater or lesser extent, throughout life. For example, during the very first stage of life, we come to learn a basic attitude about life that is mostly characterized by trust (if we were treated with consistent, responsive, care) or mistrust (if our world was chaotic and adults were capricious, unresponsive, or malevolent in their treatment of us). As we think of the array of parents who have shown up at school, we can characterize each of them along this dimension and see that there are parents who still deal with issues of trust at a basic level, and this affects the way they respond to us and to the school environment in general. We can think of other parents who are pretty trusting, but who don't seem very autonomous and independent. There are some who don't feel as competent to take initiative as we might hope, and there are some who have never quite found a way to learn and use skills that the larger culture values and rewards, thus developing a weak sense of "industry."

[handwritten margin notes: Treat parents the way you want to be treated / Trust is the most important factor for parents*]*

The hope-giving aspect of Erikson's (1963) theory is that any one of these life issues is still alive for us as adults, and therefore we can move toward a more psychologically healthy resolution at any stage of life. Thus, a counselor's interaction that fosters a greater sense of trust or autonomy or competence or personal uniqueness for a parent can create ripple effects that lead to greater psychological health in other aspects of that parent's life.

While we keep one eye on the horizon of the growth potential of the parents we interact with, we keep the other eye on the present and speak to the parent who is before us today. Our communications

Listen,
Listen,
Listen
The 3 Ls

with parents will be most effective when they are couched in ways that meet the parent where he or she is at emotionally and psychologically. I find that using Erikson's (1963) theory makes me more sensitive to particular parents and their current emotional and psychological level of development. I used it, for example, when Adriana's father, Carlos, came to school one afternoon on his day off to tell me that he didn't approve of the new academic testing procedures that had been initiated in our state. He said he felt that the testing mandates had created pressure that was detrimental to his daughter and had made her fearful of school. I think Carlos knew that he was complaining about something I couldn't change; his manner suggested that he simply felt a need to have a say about something he thought was important for his child and probably other children as well. But the anxiousness and intensity in his voice made me wonder whether there was more at stake for him than what first met the eye. So in addition to listening to his stated concern, I thought about him in terms of Erikson's (1963) stages: He was exhibiting a great deal of trust in approaching me with his perception of the problem; he was showing independent and autonomous thinking in thoughtfully taking exception to our testing practices; he had shown initiative in coming to the school and finding me. His main worry was that it was becoming harder for his daughter to come to school and feel good about learning, so I concluded that his worry had to do with keeping alive his daughter's sense of industry, or self-efficacy. I also speculated that probably, in his own school experiences, Carlos had met some serious challenges to his sense of competence when he was at this stage. To build the best communication connection with Carlos, one that would establish a working relationship that could continue beyond this present problem, I needed to address him as a whole person (with a history, with memories about his own school experiences, with his own feelings of competencies and deficiencies) who was bringing a problem to my attention. Instead of focusing exclusively on the testing issue, it was important to understand the dimensions of his self-concept that provided the backdrop for his concern about testing. Sure enough, Carlos responded positively to being heard, and he became a parent I could count on for many years.

I find that parents often rework these psychological stages as their children work through them for the first time. As Adriana encountered threats to her sense of self while at school, her father's own school memories and old feelings of inadequacy surfaced, challenging him anew. His coming to school and talking to me was a way of working once more on his sense of self-efficacy and competence in a school setting, but this time, it was as a parent. I knew I needed to acknowledge this part of Carlos that had the potential to grow in addition to acknowledging his surface complaint. By attending to Carlos at this deeper level, and keeping it in the background of my mind, I communicated to him the same message I would want to convey to his daughter, had she sought my help: I see you as an individual. I know you have a unique set of concerns that are important to you at this time. I respect your reasons for why these concerns matter to you in the way that they do right now. Even though I may never know these reasons, I will listen to you with respect and compassion and find a way to help if I can.

Certainly, there are times to become task oriented and solve problems that parents bring us as quickly and efficiently as possible. Parents appreciate it and don't forget it when we can bring our power and expertise to bear on a situation that involves their child and resolve it. For the long run, however, I believe that parents feel most at home in schools where counselors and others don't just solve problems for them but convey regard for them as unique, developing persons. Parents can feel the difference between schools where they are genuinely welcome and valued as unique people and schools where they are treated generically, important only for making sure their kids show up every day and don't cause too many problems.

Creating a Vision
for Parent Participation

No matter how dedicated we are about establishing beneficial experiences for children at school, we must never forget that the most significant part of the environment for the child lies outside the school: the child's home and family. Because we, as counselors, want to establish the best environment we can for the child, and do everything possible to ensure that child's healthy development, it makes sense for us to see the child's family as falling within our circle of care and influence.

Is this just another burden of responsibility? Not necessarily. An experienced school counselor becomes adept at delivering *mini-interventions*—a meaningful glance to this child, a special smile across a crowded hallway to another, a 3-minute session with a child on the front walkway before the school doors are open. In schools, we know that children's lives are often changed in profound ways because of the "small stuff" rather than because of the latest fashionable state-sponsored, expensive program that is supposed to cure our students' every ill.

And so it is with reaching out to parents. Rather than seeing our responsibility toward parents as an impossible burden—another program we have to design and deliver, more meetings to schedule into an already impossible day—we can choose to see our responsibility as more a matter of attitude, at least to start with, than a matter of projects and programs. We can let go of the impression that parents are yet another needy group that we must to do something *to* or *for.* Instead, we can see our responsibility as primarily building the bridge, knowing that others after us will use the bridge to accomplish things we don't even have time to dream of! We can trust that if we build a bridge of goodwill, then many, if not all, parents will find the school a good place to come.

If we truly believe that all parents are competent to participate in their children's education, and that parent involvement communicates to children that they matter, we will be genuine in welcoming any contact with a parent or guardian (even if it starts off as angry, adversarial contact!). I know one counselor whose primary message to parents is, "I work for *you.* You tell me what you hope for and dream of for your child. My job is to work with you to make it happen." She is defining herself, up front, as a team member with the parent, not an authority or adversary. On hearing this message for the first time, many parents are uncomprehending, stunned. No school teacher or administrator has treated them in this empowering way before! She repeats it: "Yes, I see myself as working for you. Now, what would you like for us to accomplish?" She says she loves to see their shock and then the dawn of possibilities on their faces.

The first step in creating more vital involvement with parents is to examine our vision of who parents are and what they can do. As professionals, we know that having a limited vision of a child's capabilities or a diminished view of how far that child can go will, sure enough, tend to come true. So we strive always to keep before us a sense of the capabilities the child does have, the many things the child has learned and will learn, the contributions the child does make to his or her family, school, and peers. Let's extend this "possibilities thinking" to parents and caregivers, and ask ourselves, Have we been unnecessarily limited in how we see these adults? Have we focused on their potential, as well as their shortcomings? Have we overlooked the competencies they do have, in our frustration with the competencies they don't seem to have? Have we focused only on what they cost us, in time and energy, rather than noticing the rich information they bring about what it means to live in their world? Have we been genuinely respectful of the contributions they make to their families and open to their participation in the schools?

More than any other parent I've known, Toni taught me not to underestimate the changes a parent might be capable of making, given a lot of personal determination and a little support from the schools. I'll never forget the day Toni came to school to enroll her oldest son, Marcus, in kindergarten. With her baby daughter on her hip, Toni sat down to fill out the many forms. Marcus proceeded to turn my office into a three-ring circus, all by himself! I have never before or since encountered a child whose behavior was so erratic and so rapidly changing in such a short space of time. He turned my trash can upside down and stood on it; he ran from one side of the room to the other; he hid behind my desk; he bit the head off one of my toys. Toni looked up and confessed to me that Marcus wasn't entirely potty trained. My heart sank when I imagined the reaction of the teacher I would assign to him.

Sure enough, it was a very challenging year. The teachers were soon circulating rumors they had heard about Toni and her husband, Julio, moving to our state to escape drug charges facing them in the northeast. Julio, with his beard, long hair, and tattoos, had Marcus's teacher muttering that she would never again eat at the restaurant where he had gotten a job as a cook. Toni inspired more confidence—

she had received her GED and gone back to college to take a few courses—but there were times when Marcus's teachers came to me with hot discussions about whether or not to file child abuse complaints (due to many and frequent bruises on Marcus's body) or child neglect allegations (from the apparently unsupervised scrapes he got himself into, like the bad tangle he once had with a cactus patch).

Toni's strong point was that she always brought Marcus to school herself; she always walked him into the building. She was curious about what was going on, and she used that occasion to ask questions. To her credit, she had an apparently thick skin, and she ignored the air of superiority we must have exuded at times. Gradually, as teachers made suggestions to her about how to work with Marcus, Toni became a more effective parent. By the end of the year, she had inspired our admiration for her determination to understand her child and build a better life for herself and her family. Marcus managed to graduate to the first grade (and was, by then, completely potty trained). But the family moved across town about that time, having found a better neighborhood, so I lost track of them.

Several years later, while visiting a nearby school, I happened on Toni in the school hallway. She was delighted to see me and to share her good news: She had graduated from college. Julio had gotten a better job. Both her children were in school now and doing fine. But even more inspiring to me was the news that Toni was the PTA president for that year. Her enthusiasm, as she shared with me some of her innovative ideas for reaching out to parents and involving them in the organization, warmed my heart. "I will never forget how you all taught me so much that first year," she said. "I learned so much from you." Actually, I was the one who learned a lot this time. When I remembered the dismal forecast we had for her, for her child, and for her family, I was ashamed. I resolved never again to underestimate what a parent might be preparing to do. No formal parenting program changed Toni; we had simply made ourselves available to her, over and over again, and she had taken what she needed to make her life a better one. Now, in turn, she was reaching out to others and was, I'll bet, very effective in inspiring other parents to get involved on behalf of their kids.

In conclusion, then, the answer to "Why bother?" is that reaching out to parents can become one of the most rewarding parts of our job. When we look each parent in the eyes as a person of unfolding potential, from whom we have much to learn, with whom we can team up to get some good things done, we ready ourselves for all sorts of constructive possibilities.

2

Tools and Techniques for Building Bridges

S chool counselors would be ecstatic if more parents came to school, asked questions, volunteered to help out. And there are always some parents who bring their child to school and who stay, who enjoy being involved, and who keep closely in touch with their child's teachers and counselor. But this is not the norm. How, specifically, can we reach out for that parent who seems to be reluctant to have contact with us? Who has more fears than hopes for his or her child's school experience?

Rosa is a school counselor in a small community where parents are seldom seen or heard. Many of the children in her school are from migrant families who have come to work in agriculturally related enterprises. She describes her experience:

14

My first year, I was simply in shock. These children were so needy. Where were their parents? As time passed, I found myself becoming angrier and angrier at these invisible and uncaring (so I thought) parents. But my second year, something happened that I'll never forget. It changed the way that I understand their lack of involvement.

I had "bus duty" that day, meaning I was responsible for staying outside and supervising the school grounds until all the children left. It was windy and freezing outside—a cold front just blowing through, you know, and I couldn't wait for my duty to be over so I could go home. When nearly everyone was gone, I noticed a little shadow of a kid hanging around behind me. "Time to go home," I encouraged. He just looked back at me. "Did you forget something in the building?" I guessed. But he shook his head. "Miss your bus?" Wrong again. "Well, it's time to go home, you see; all the kids are gone and it is time for me to leave too." I tried to sound kind but insistent. Then I saw his eyes filling with big tears. I knelt down to talk to him and noticed then that he was shivering and he had no coat—in this weather! "Hey, what's up? Where's your coat? Let's go inside to talk about it—I'm freezing, so you must feel like an ice cube!"

In a really soft voice I could barely hear, he said, "Miss, I don't want to go home because I have to walk and it is so cold. Miss, don't make me walk home. I just want to stay here. Can I just stay here?" Well, by now my heart was breaking for this little guy and I would have done anything for him. I said, "No, you can't stay here, but I tell you what, I'll make sure you get a coat, and I'll take you home myself so you won't have to walk." And I'll give your mama a piece of my mind while I'm at it, I said to myself!

We went by the Used Duds store and we found him a $2 special that fit him just fine. Then he told me the way and we got out to the farm where his family was staying in a drafty little house. When his mom opened the door, and I saw the terrified look on her face, I had to swallow the scolding speech I had been preparing. Luckily, the boy took over and explained to her that I was just there on a mission of mercy. When she saw the coat he was wearing, she took my hand in heartfelt thanks. She offered me some coffee and I stayed awhile, and we visited in broken English and Spanish while several young toddlers climbed in and out of our laps. When I stood up to go, she took my hand again. "Oh Miss," she whispered, "thank you. When I was in school the teachers were not nice to us. I see you are nice to my son and the other children. Thank you."

That's how I got started in the coat business. Now in the spring, all the kids bring me their coats that they've outgrown and don't need anymore. I keep a big box outside my office, and they made some space for me down at the bus barn so I can store them over the summer. In the fall, when new families come to the school, I make sure every child has a coat to wear when cold weather comes. These families don't understand how cold it can get up here in the winter! Oh, I know, some people say, "What's a school counselor doing in the coat business?" But that's how I build a bridge to my families. Most migrant parents have had their share of bad experiences with schools. So I have to do something that shows them I really care about the welfare of their child. This is the best way I've found to open the door.

Rosa found an effective way to build bridges to the hard-to-reach parents in her community by trying out a creative and unconventional solution that puts her in contact with families and lets them know of her helpful intentions. Yes, it takes some time and involves many after-school trips to the bus barn, but it also gives her opportunities for contacts with children and parents that are not problem focused. Rosa finds that the payoff is worth her energy because it establishes a relationship and paves the way for later interaction about school issues. Coats give Rosa and her families a common ground of trust. Certainly, a coats for kids program isn't the answer for every school counselor. But the good news is that there are many creative ways to build bridges. In fact, the best bridges are built to suit the local environmental demands—those are particular to the setting; there is no one-size-fits-all bridge design that could work for every river in the continent.

Because bridge building takes time and effort, it is an activity that bears certain costs for the counselor. So it is a project that is likely to be abandoned unless the counselor is clear about why the bridge is needed, what kind of bridge is needed, what will be needed to build the bridge, and how the needed bridge-building materials will be procured. Chapter 1 addresses the "why"; this chapter addresses the "how": the techniques of bridge building.

Planning the Bridge:
What Is the Goal?

Bridge building is about taking steps to bring yourself closer to parents, especially parents who are tough to reach. In these cases, it is the counselor who must make the first move. (One kind of parent who usually makes the first move to build a bridge toward us is discussed in Chapter 3.) Planning a bridge that will accomplish its purpose is facilitated by asking the following questions.

Do You Want the Bridge to Bear
Two-Way Traffic or One-Way Traffic?

Some counselors believe that their primary role with parents is to deliver information. In this case, counselors will not be concerned with building a bridge wide enough to bear two-way traffic. Sometimes, the information delivery function is clearly the most important in a particular situation, such as when the counselor is letting parents know about registration procedures, application deadlines, testing policies, or program requirements. But if information delivery is all that is done, the counselor misses opportunities to make a team member out of a parent. Parents who are approached as individuals who have information the schools need to benefit children, as people with very valuable contributions to make, and whose help is needed to solve school problems are more likely to become involved and stay involved in school life. So, just as transportation authorities know, two-way bridges are always preferable if there are enough resources to build them. (But in the press of time demands that many school counselors face every day, a one-way bridge to most parents is all that is possible, and this is better than no bridge at all.)

How Heavy Will the Loads Be
That the Bridge Will Need to Bear?

Do you anticipate needing a bridge that will accommodate only light traffic, such as informing parents about special programs, schedule planning, and scholarship opportunities? Or will the bridge be needed for heavier traffic, like working with parents to be sure their special-needs child has the necessary accommodations? Those children who have a history of discipline problems at school probably require the most substantial bridge of all, if the counselor is going to be able to keep in touch with the parents and maintain a spirit of teamwork and problem solving.

How Extensive Is the Distance
That Will Need to Be Bridged?

Do the counselor and the parents speak the same language? Are there chasms of cultural differences that must be crossed? Are parents recent immigrants who have very limited knowledge about how schools operate in this country?

When architects design bridges that must span great distances, they plan ways in which the bridge itself has additional support. When cultural gaps are wide, school counselors need to find additional support for bridging to these parents—otherwise, it is precisely these families who will drop through the cracks because they are difficult to reach with conventional methods of communication.

Some counselors have found it helpful to strike up a relationship with another parent or employee at the school who has a language or a background similar to the culturally or linguistically different child's family. Even before the counselor approaches the parents, he or she can ask this informant for insights about what might be important for understanding this family. During meetings, this support person can literally or figuratively "speak the same language" as the family and help make sure the family and counselor genuinely understand each other.

Hilda is a bilingual Hispanic counselor who is adept at building bridges to families emigrating from Central and South American countries, but she admits that she is at a loss when it comes to reaching out to Haitian and other island immigrants. Although Hilda considers herself a multicultural expert, she is adamant that she must have some backup when working with the families of students with a culture and language unfamiliar to her. "It's the only way I can ethically serve these people," she says, "and they have a right to the same information, the same help, as anyone else. How can I give them that unless I have someone who can translate between their world and mine?" Hilda cultivates relationships with as many people as she can find who are bicultural members of marginal groups, who can translate back and forth between the various Caribbean dialects and English or Spanish, and she calls on their volunteer assistance when she needs it.

Clearing and Leveling the Ground: Removing Barriers

The counselor-parent relationship is, like any relationship, built over time. Sometimes it develops naturally and almost effortlessly, but at other times it requires the counselor's intentional effort. Sometimes there is resistance that must be overcome—on the part of both the counselor and the parent. But let's face it: We counselors are professionals, and we are being paid to build bridges. It follows, then, that we must take the lead and be the most energetic about finding a way to span the gaps.

Sometimes we get the feeling that the air between us and a parent is thick. Nothing seems to be working despite our efforts and enthusiasm. At these times, subtle cultural differences between counselor and client may be having a chilling effect on the communication climate. We all make innocent mistakes occasionally that leave us with a vague sense of lack of connection. Christine recalls an enlightening moment she had. She had asked Tom's advice for making better connections with the American Indian and Hispanic families she worked with in New Mexico. Christine, trying hard to fulfill all her professional duties, had scheduled a day of back-to-back home visits for all the special needs students at her school. She conscientiously tried to build bridges to these parents ... but she had a feeling they all had collapsed! "What did I do wrong?" she asked Tom, a native from the area. He laughed. "You went in there with an outline, right, and got down to business?" "Yes," Christine affirmed. "And you didn't take your time, have a little something to eat, chitchat with them first, right?" "Oh no," Christine said. "I told them I didn't want to waste their time, so I'd get right to the point. And I don't want to eat that stuff they offer me, so I just say 'no, thank you.' " "Big mistake!" Tom laughed. "You see this belly on me? This is an occupational hazard for counselors around here, if you know what you're doing. You see, it is very rude to get right down to business before asking after the family and maybe having a little something to eat together. Beginning with some of these civilities is our way of showing respect. I guess it helps us keep problems and bureaucracies in a human perspective." Christine felt quite embarrassed about her innocent faux pas, but resolved to slow down and work up her courage to partake of some new foods when they were offered. Tom gave her some other good advice: "Instead of coming in and jumping into your agenda, Christine, take some time for you and the parents to acclimate to each other. Follow their lead for a while. Then, after a respectful number of exchanges, you can begin talking about what *you* need to talk about."

A different problem that requires some soul-searching honesty is the presence of negative beliefs and emotions that affect our ability to respond with compassion to particular children and their parents. "I have to admit it," Sam confessed. "I had a really hard time with the kids in my school of Middle Eastern or Arab descent. Every time I saw one of their parents, I had one thought: terrorists! Even though I knew this was probably unfair, I think I really believed that all Middle-Easterners must be involved in some kind of subversive activity. But one year I really got to know this Muslim family. I learned an incredible amount, and seeing them up close taught me how wrong I was." To Sam's credit, he realized that the best antidote was to approach exactly the kind of people for whom he had prejudiced feelings and seek to know them better.

Sometimes we see ourselves as having overcome racial or ethnic biases, but there may be other kinds of biases that we are allowing to get in the way. Our own pet peeve might be parents who are in motorcycle gangs. Or parents who are lawyers. Or parents who are atheists, or fundamentalists. Or ones we suspect of having trouble with drugs, or the law, or ones who seem to have a lot more money than we do. It is worth checking ourselves over for these potential obstacles. Are there groups of parents we are really willing to mark off our list as "unreachables"? Sometimes we act as if there are, even though we might deny it.

Another factor can affect the counselor's efforts to build bridges to "different" families, and this one is not directly under the counselor's control. Unfortunately, even in this age of multiculturalism, some school personnel think (and worse, say) disparaging things about the background and culture of a child's home environment. Even when these opinions are not overtly shared, both the child and the caregivers pick up on the unspoken message. I recently visited a school on the Navajo reservation in Arizona. Although I was very impressed with the professional commitment of many of the individuals working there—Navajo, Hispanic, Anglo, and those of mixed race—there was one nonnative teacher who surprised me by murmuring disparaging remarks about "these people" under her breath. Her attitude stood in marked contrast to the others'. My curiosity was whetted. This was a beautiful but very remote area—a place one couldn't move to without effort. "Why are you here?" I asked her, when I had a chance to talk with her over lunch. "Oh, I wanted to get my kids as far away from my ex-husband as I could," was her reply. "It worked. He would have nothing to do with this place." Clearly, this teacher's prejudiced attitudes could undermine the others' most sensitive efforts to gain the trust of families. Sometimes the counselor's efforts are best directed toward acknowledging and seeking to resolve the cultural or racial tensions that exist within individuals or groups of individuals in the school—a tall order, but the alternative is to acquiesce to a harmful status quo.

Some counselors interpret parents' lack of involvement as indicating a lack of concern for the child, or as their way of devaluing the whole educational process. Holding on to these negative assumptions about parents makes bridge building harder: Any motions a counselor may go through to invite involvement will feel inauthentic (and therefore suspicious) to the family. It is more constructive, then, to step back and look for other reasons to explain parents' reluctance to interact with school professionals. Here is a sampling of reasons that have affected some parents:

- Many parents have memories of being shamed or discouraged during their school days. Recently, a grandfather who had become involved in a school literacy program for his young granddaughter disclosed to the counselor that when he was growing up in a migrant family in the Southwest, his parents placed him in school for the first time, and because of his age he ended up in a second-grade classroom. On his first day, his teacher told him to stand and write a sentence on the board. Because this was his first school experience, he could not comply. He was also too terrified to explain himself because he knew little English, so he was spanked for being defiant. Returning home that day, he begged his parents not to make him go back to school. They agreed. Now, he said, he was very surprised and pleased to see that a school could create a different kind of experience from what he had. But it had taken him nearly 40 years to overcome his fear of walking into a school building!

- Parents may feel ambivalent about another social institution having so much power in their child's life. This may be particularly true if the school is seen as an active agent of assimilation, pressuring children to "lose their culture." These fears set up an "us versus them" wariness, which counselors must work hard to counteract. In Miami, for example, high school counselors who encourage daughters from Cuban American families to aim for college scholarships at faraway universities are seen as creating trouble by those parents who want their adult children, especially their daughters, to remain geographically close.

- Parents may be afraid that if they openly differ with a teacher or the school, their child will be discriminated against. In some families, stories of repression and retaliation for taking exception to the rules of "the authorities" are painfully fresh. Like it or not, the school counselor is seen by these adults as just another of the authorities at the school—someone with the power to turn them in or make life more difficult for their child. These parents keep their distance or, when they do show up, say as little as possible, trying to reveal nothing.

▓ Many parents think no news is good news—they believe they'll have to talk to you only if a problem comes up (and they pray it won't). This makes sense when you realize that parent involvement is a relatively recent goal in the schools. Back when many of today's parents were in school, their own parents were discouraged from being involved. Schools sent a nonverbal message to families that said, "Leave the educating to us— we're the professionals!"

▓ Some families struggle with work schedules that prohibit their presence at daytime or evening functions. Some parents hold two jobs, simply trying to meet their family's most basic needs. These parents are already stretched to the limit, but their lack of participation does not necessarily mean lack of interest.

▓ Some parents have already had negative interactions with school personnel about their child. Deep in their hearts, these parents fervently hope that the school professionals will like their child and think he or she is doing well. But they're afraid that any day now they'll find out otherwise. Any note, any phone call, any counselor saying, "We need to talk," means trouble. So these parents are elusive, hoping to postpone hearing more bad news about their child.

With all these obstacles, what can be done to clear the way?

The most essential ingredient to a more satisfying relationship between school professionals and family caregivers is that the counselor have the child's welfare truly at heart and that he or she be genuinely concerned about the child. This genuine concern must come across to the parents. When parents can see and feel that this is true, trust will grow and the bridge between home and school can be built.

Counselors and schools express that they are genuinely concerned about a child in many ways. When the child is reasonably happy at the end of a school day, the parent senses that the child has been in good hands. When the counselor makes a comment such as, "I've seen Amanda in the halls this year; she seems to have so many friends," the parent knows that the counselor has been paying some attention to the child. When, during private conferences with parents, counselors share snapshot pictures of the child or anecdotes of school life that involve the child, or show the parent some of the child's drawings (with the child's permission, of course), parents know that this counselor takes their child personally! When the counselor has organized ways to find test results or records about the student, then parents know that the welfare of their individual child is one of the counselor's primary concerns. When parents see the counselor speak to their child with friendly affection, barriers break down. Trust clears the way.

Building the Bridge: Gaining Cooperation

First Contact With Parents

Whenever possible, a counselor's first contact with the parents needs to occur before a problem phone call is necessary. This is especially important for those whose children have had trouble in the past, those who associate communication from the school with hearing more bad news about their child. The goal is establish some rapport with the parents—to build the bridge and test it out a little before it needs to bear a heavy load.

One way to do this is to contact parents early on to say hello and to report some good—or at least neutral—news about their child. For example, when a counselor gets the file of a child that is already stuffed with "pink slips" from past skirmishes, he or she can call and say something like this:

"Hello, I'm _____. I am the counselor for Shandra this year at school. I just wanted to introduce myself and let you know that I've talked with her about the schedule change she's requested. I think we're going to be able to work out something so she can get the electives she wants."

Suppose Shandra's father alludes to her troubled past. "I thought you'd be calling to tell me Shandra's in trouble already!" he might say. Because he's brought up the issue of her past school problems, you could acknowledge that, too, and lay a foundation for some teamwork. You might say, "Yes, I've got Shandra's file here, and I notice that she's been through some challenging times in the past, as far as school goes. Could you tell me your view of what Shandra needs to have a good year at school? I'd really like to be helpful, if I can."

This kind of talk communicates that you see yourself as on the same side as the parent, not in opposition. It invites parents to share their perspective, and their perspective is a key piece to your understanding of their child, so when a parent opens up to you at this point, it is as good as gold.

Next, you might ask, "What are your hopes for Shandra this year?" (This is also a good place to start when contacting parents of children who don't come to a counselor with a troubled school history.) When parents collaborate with you to think about what they want to happen for the child, these *shared goals can be used to forge a cooperative relationship between parents and school professionals.* When a counselor genuinely asks, "What do you really want for your child, both short range and long range?" then a point of alliance can be found.

A caution is in order, however. Parents have radar for detecting condescending or cynical attitudes in school professionals. Depending on their history, they may carry with them a healthy dose of suspicion of a counselor who sounds too good to be true. You might have to try more than once, but with determination, you will find that most parents come around and enjoy talking about how they see their child's strengths and ways they'd like to see their child doing better. Parents will open up when they sense that you really value their opinion of what they want for their child's future.

Ideally, you will form an alliance with a parent that fosters this sort of genuine dialogue. Before you end the conversation, ask the parents if they'd like to formulate some goals for the coming semester that you might be able to help out with. Aim toward concreteness. Identify a few very specific—and realistic—goals to target. This may take some discussion, because the most helpful goals will be those that you can, in some way, measure, and those that offer a good chance for actual success.

For example, suppose you've called a parent whose middle-school son was absent more than he was present last year. As a result, his grades suffered, and he was kicked off the basketball team. When you ask this parent about her hopes for next year, she says she wants her boy to "stay out of trouble" and her long-range goal is for him to "graduate and make money playing ball." These are great goals, but they are too general for a short-term focus. Maybe you even think playing ball is out of reach for this kid, given what you've observed about his body build and apparent lack of innate talent. But both of you can agree on the fact that getting through eighth grade and staying on the team all year are the next step to take up the ladder. Those are the broad goals for the year. From there, work together to pull out plausible, measurable goals that have a high probability for success in the short run. For example, the counselor and this parent might agree that, during the first 6 weeks of school, they want the boy to have fewer absences than he had during the previous spring semester and passing grades in every class so he can keep athletic eligibility. (For additional suggestions on setting goals, see Sklare, 1997.)

Once the goals have been established, explain that parental support is critical. For example, you might say, "I'll talk to the teachers, and we'll do our part, but it won't happen without your help, too." Try to get a specific offer from the parent of how he or she will contribute to reaching the goals. This part of the conversation might go like this:

"So, we agreed that fewer absences would be good. I guess you're the one who is going to have the most influence on that one. What do you think would help Xavier be at school more days during the first 6 weeks?"

"Well, I have thought of getting him his own alarm clock. . . . "

"Yes, great! He's at a good age to be responsible for getting himself up. But what about when he doesn't want to get up . . . says he doesn't feel good, and goes back to sleep?"

"I'm not sure. I hate to force him to go if he really doesn't feel good. But I've noticed he seems to start feeling good every afternoon about when the other kids get out of school."

"What does Xavier do on the days he doesn't make it to school?"

"Oh, he says he's sick, so he sleeps late, but then he usually watches some TV and then goes out after a while."

"So it sounds like skipping school is a lot more fun than going to school. Who could blame him? On this end, I can work on making sure he has a better day when he's at school. But I wonder if it would also help if you made it less fun to stay at home?"

"Yeah . . . maybe I've been spoiling him a little on this one."

"Maybe. Some parents I know make a rule like, 'If you're too sick for school you're too sick for anything else. So no going out with your friends; you have to stay home and rest in bed and eat chicken soup!' "

"Or I could say if he's sick then we have to get up and go to the clinic and try to see a doctor. He hates sitting in the clinic."

"Right. But if he's really sick, then that's where he needs to be."

"Or if he just oversleeps and doesn't want to go to school for some reason, then I could take him over to work at his grandfather's shop for the rest of the day. Instead of TV."

"Exactly. It's not mean, it just lets Xavier know how important it is to you that he stays well and stays in school, and that you're going to stay on top of the situation."

Once you and the parent have agreed on some ideas about how to work toward the goals, let the parent know that you intend to stay in touch. You might say, "I'll be calling now and then so you can let me know how things are going at home, and I can let you know how things are going at school. At the end of the 6 weeks, let's sit down with Xavier and compare his absences and his grades to last year's to see if we are making progress."

Conclude by expressing confidence that things will go well: "I have great hopes for Xavier. I'm going to meet with Xavier soon and get his ideas, too, about how to make this a better year for him."

Using and Maintaining the Bridge:
Parent Contacts, Conferences, and Consultations

To maintain a good bridge, regular, positive interaction with parents must be a priority! To maintain a working alliance that both of you have faith in, it is very important to maintain a balance of communication that is as much about noticing and celebrating successes as it is about identifying problems.

Watch for the first sign of success—and then make a positive contact. One way to do this is by building it into your daily routine. Some counselors have the personal goal of making at least one positive contact—by phone, by note, or in person—each day. These routine, solution-focused contacts are brief, describe a positive behavior as specifically as possible, and express how the counselor feels (e.g., encouraged, proud, happy).

Keeping a brief log to document these contacts is one way to let you see evidence that you are reaching your goal of increasing the amount of positive contact with parents. It is also a way of checking yourself to be sure you're fair—that you're spreading your attention to all types of students, not more of one gender or culture.

Other possibilities for positive contact include the following:

- Checking on absences in a way that shows that you care—a "get well" phone call or "we've missed you" postcard. (Student office assistants in middle and high schools can be trained to address and mail your correspondence.)

- Dashing off "one-liner" notes or postcards to children for the merest of excuses—keep a stack in your date book and send off a few when you end up "on hold" or get stuck in a long meeting. "I saw how you helped Miss Ramsey the other day with her big stack of boxes. Way to go! Kids like you make our school a good place to be." Although these notes or postcards aren't addressed specifically to parents, they are tangible evidence that you know their child and you see the good in him or her.

- Making the most of casual opportunities when you encounter families at community events—greeting children with warmth and enthusiasm when you run into them at the grocery store or the football game. It warms parents' hearts to see a school professional genuinely pleased to see their child.

When you get in the habit of making positive contacts, the contacts to report a problem won't be so difficult—for you or the parent. But, inevitably, those days do come. Children have bad days at school—or bad weeks, or bad semesters. The school counselor must decide when to involve the parents.

One helpful point to remember is that parents need not be informed about every skirmish that takes place between children or between children and their teachers. First of all, there isn't time to do this; second, spending this much time being problem focused will derail your other efforts at keeping the bridge between you and parents trustworthy and inviting. Some counselors find that the popular Your Own Child test is a good way to sort out which problems require parent attention, in addition to the attention of school staff. Here is how the Your Own Child test works:

▓ Assume you have a child the age of the child involved.
▓ If your child was doing the behavior, would you want a call?
▓ If yes, call. If no, then don't.

Most of us would want to know if the problem behavior was becoming more frequent or more intense or seemed to be developing into a pattern that interfered with our child's success at school. Most of us would not want to know the blow-by-blow account of how our child said "fart" in gym class and set off ripples of laughter that resulted in an unpleasant confrontation with the teacher. Of course, this rule of thumb doesn't apply to every case. Sometimes demands from other school professionals or ethical considerations require us to make the call, regardless.

Problem phone calls follow the same approach as positive contacts but require a little more planning:

▓ Outline the points you wish to make. You might want to use the Parent Conference Planning Sheet (Figure 2.1) to help you

Child's name _____ Conference date _____

Parent(s) name(s) _____ Time _____

Counselor's name _____

1. Example of child's unique qualities:

_____

_____

2. Past concerns to be updated at the conference:

_____

_____

3. Strengths of the child:

_____

_____

4. If appropriate, areas of concern or delayed development:

_____

_____

5. Parent input on child's progress: _____

_____

6. Goals for the student for the rest of the year:

_____

_____

Suggestions for action at school:

Suggestions for action at home:

Additional conference notes:

Figure 2.1. Parent Conference Planning Sheet

SOURCE: *Building Bridges With Parents,* by Marilyn T. Montgomery. Copyright 1999 by Corwin Press.

remember to point out the child's strengths as well as the current problems. This will help both you and the parent keep the problem in perspective and remain solution focused.

▪ Use the parent's language—or get a translator.

▪ Be brief. Stick to one issue.

▪ Describe the problem behavior as specifically as possible.

▪ Express how you feel about it (e.g., troubled, puzzled, concerned, worried).

▪ Request what you need the parent to do next.

▪ Clearly state what you need to do next, and commit to it.

▪ Ask for feedback to be sure you have a mutual understanding.

▪ *Important*: Document this contact in the child's file.

Other conferences and consultations that involve the parents often follow prespecified agendas. Sometimes these meetings are tension filled for both the parent and the school professionals involved. In these cases, the counselor's bridge-maintaining skills are more valuable and more needed than ever. Sometimes this means that the counselor works hard throughout the meeting to reframe problem statements into solution-focused statements. Sometimes it means using all of one's skills to foster a true spirit of collaboration and teamwork among the parent and the others involved. Sometimes it means leaving a conference with an unparalleled sense of gratification from knowing you've made a difference, or with a sense of awe from experiencing the power of group process at its best. Unfortunately, it also sometimes means watching bridges you've worked hard to build blow up in your face. The experienced counselor knows that that's an inevitable part of doing business. But when the smoke clears, it is time to get back to work.

3

Troubled Kids, Anxious Parents

When a counselor contacts parents because a child's problems have been increasing in frequency or intensity, the parent often has already been concerned about the child for some time. Parents' anxiety about their child may be at an all-time high, and their confidence in their own ability to parent effectively may be at an all-time low. A crisis event at school may precipitate the counselor's phone call, but at home, parents have probably already been feeling a rising sense of trouble and anxiousness.

With some families, the counselor never has to figure out how to build a bridge; the parents already have concerns about their child and therefore seek to make the counselor their ally. These chronically anxious parents create a different set of issues for the child and the counselor, for sometimes the problem is not how to reach them and get them involved, but how to get them to relax a little and give you and their child some space.

Anxiety is a normal and even functional emotion associated with parenting. The renowned pediatrician T. Berry Brazelton (1992) writes about parents' early emotional reactions to a new child:

> Together with this delight will be a natural anxiety. All parents who care deeply will be anxious. Anxiety serves a vital purpose: calling up energy to help parents meet new responsibilities. Anxiety can open them up to the [child] and to others who can help them. (p. 37)

He adds, however, that "if anxiety is overwhelming, it can close off new parents or lead to depression. A depressed new parent is no longer available to the many cues the [child] offers" (p. 38)

Having some low-level anxiety increases parents' attentiveness to their kids, but anxiety swamps them when it becomes too intense. When parents are "at the end of their rope" with a child, their anxiety has usually risen to the point that they are closing themselves off from other resources and are too tense to detect the many cues that the child or adolescent offers in the current situation. So things get worse. Often, this anxious escalation began as a natural, beneficial response to an alarming event (such as serious illness, a brush with the law, a death in the family). Cycles of rising anxiety can become chronic, however. At this point, the continued "alarm reaction" of the parent, although originally helpful in meeting a crisis, becomes debilitating and interferes with the ability of the child to restabilize. Worry and anxiousness move some parents into rigid, inflexible beliefs and behaviors with their children, exacerbating problems even further. Other parents respond to feeling worried by disengaging from the child or by swinging chaotically from being overcontrolling to throwing their hands in the air and giving up.

Some parents are anxious, and for good reason: Their child or teen is truly in trouble. Our job, with respect to these parents, is to channel their anxiety into constructive action rather than blame, to keep them engaged in problem solving on behalf of their kids.

Other parents, however, are chronically anxious for no reason that we can infer from the child's behavior. These parents tend to show up often, make demands, and worry constantly that something with their child or with the school is going wrong. This chapter provides some new ways to think about both of these types of anxious parents, and offers some suggestions for moderating their anxiety back to a healthy level of responsiveness and concern.

Parents' Themes of Anxiety

Narrative therapy, a counseling perspective growing in popularity, suggests that parental anxiety (whether related to a precipitating incident on the part of their child or not) can be distilled into a theme or story line. Anxiety escalates when a child behaves in ways that might contradict or belie the family story. Below are examples of common anxious story themes. Following a look at these themes, I offer some antidotes that counselors have found to be effective for calming down adults so they can be better parents.

The Overindulgent Story

"We want only the best opportunities for my child even if it bankrupts the family." These parents show up at the counselor's door to insist that their child get the best classes, the best third-grade teacher, special services from the most highly qualified people in the school district, the starring role in the class play, and so forth. You also sometimes see one of these parents hustling their kindergartner off to ballet lessons or soccer practice every day, almost before the last bell has rung.

Families writing overindulgent stories leave their children vulnerable to something that has whimsically been termed *affluenza,* which is the malaise that develops when children are handed too many material opportunities without any effort on their own part. When adults make children the exclusive focal point of their lives and do everything for them or give them everything, these children are denied an opportunity to develop a sense of their own efficacy. They often become chronic underfunctioners in response to their parents' overfunctioning. Counselors realize that parents' diligent efforts to remove all material obstacles from their child's life leave no challenges for the child to encounter. Children need challenges to construct a sense of personal hardiness.

The Underconfident Apprehensive Story

"I am just not equipped to deal with this child. I am sure I am ruining her life." These parents see every parenting decision as an opportunity for failure—a failure with permanent, negative consequences that will reach far into the future. Every difficulty their child has is a sure sign to them that they did something wrong or failed to do something any normal parent would have known to do. For these adults, parenting is a mysterious set of skills that appears to come more naturally to everyone else. When faced with making a decision, these parents become paralyzed with anxiety—"But what if I send her to the magnet school and it turns out to be the wrong thing?" Every choice takes on the magnitude of a life-or-death drama. Counselors often see children soaking up this kind of anxiety like a sponge, unfortunately becoming underconfident and apprehensive themselves.

The "We Are Our Own Best Friends" Story

"Our family does everything together. We really believe in our family. We don't know why other people think our child might have a problem." This is the theme of families that systems theorists call *enmeshed*. Unfortunately, these parents tend to be blind to ways in which one child may be acting out feelings of significant loneliness or alienation, not togetherness! They become defensive when anyone suggests that someone in the family might have a problem that the family can't handle. When the pressure is on, they close ranks. "We can handle it ourselves, thank you," they say, often quite convincingly.

One time a teacher reported seeing the 1-year-old child of one of our school families left, crying, in the family car as a punishment for being fussy. When he saw this happen the fourth or fifth time, he came to talk over the issues with me and decided that, in all good conscience, he had to call the child abuse hotline. The parents were stunned when a child protective services agent came and investigated. Certain that the school was involved somehow, they came to see me. "Why did you let someone dishonor us like this?" they asked. "You don't know who we are. You don't know how famous our parents are in our home community. You don't know that we are leaders in our church."

"You are right," I acknowledged, "there's a lot I don't know about you. But I think the issue is that someone saw your daughter being disciplined in a way that was psychologically and physically dangerous to her, and they want to help make sure you know other ways to work with your kids."

"That's nobody's business but ours," they insisted. "Everything is fine with us. We can handle it."

Sadly, these parents (like many others involved in child abuse investigations) closed this chapter by moving to a new community at their earliest opportunity. The counselor's worry, when encountering this type of family, is whether the well-being of the individual child is being sacrificed so that the family can go on with its success story.

The "You Will Bring Honor to the Family" Story

"We just want our son to live up to his potential and understand that our choice of teachers will affect his future medical career." In this family, the child has been cast in the role of rising star while the adults hope to one day bask in the glow. The parents have many expectations for the success of this child. They often also have a specific range of interests that they see as worthy for developing in their child. Like the young couple in the Steve Martin movie *Parenthood*, these anxious parents are determined, by the diligence of their own efforts, to raise a superstar. They see their child as entirely a product of his or her environment. They await the day when their child, the superstar, graciously acknowledges them in his or her Emmy/Pulitzer prize/ sports hall of fame/country club recognition speech: "Thank you, Mom and Dad, for making me what I am."

When encountering these parents, the counselor is concerned about how much leeway there is for the child to unfold according to his or her own developmental timetable and unique, innate interests. Without a chance to be known, valued, and accepted for who he or she is, a child usually becomes either overly compliant or, later, oppositional and defiant.

The "You Will Not Be Different" Story

This story is about the value of intergenerational continuity. There are two versions. One seeks to keep children from being more successful than the parents: "If it was good enough for us, it's good enough for you, so don't get any big ideas." The other version insists that the children must achieve the same level as the parents: "We did it, so you will, too."

If the child persists in being different in ways the family sees as troublesome, the parents first try everything they know to get the child back in line. But if the child persists in being different, one popular version families use for explaining this is the "genetic failure" theme: "There must be something wrong with this child's genes. Look at all the rest of our kids. They turned out normal. So this problem is clearly not our fault. It must be because of that [fill in the blank with a category the family finds undesirable] great-grandma married a few generations ago."

This story is especially hard for counselors to work with when it seems to them that the ways in which the child is different are valuable. Often, clashes of cultural values between certain family members and the school create these tensions.

The "You Will Be Different" Story

"I'm scared to death he's going to do what I did." The parent with abandoned hopes and dreams or some skeletons in the closet is terrified that history will repeat itself in the child. "But I'm going to nip this in the bud!" this parent determines at the first sign of trouble. So, the mother who became a parent while still a teen becomes hypervigilant when her daughter stays after school to work on a library project with a group of friends, or the father whispers a threat,

"I'll beat the tar out of you when we get home!" to a child who gets into trouble with a particularly nettlesome teacher (whom, if the truth be known, everyone finds nettlesome!). With the specter of their own past before them, it is hard for these parents to see their child's behavior in a benign light. They overreact as a way of compensating for their own past mistakes, assuming that what is going on with their child is their own history beginning to repeat itself. They become insensitive to the real here-and-now issues that their child is facing.

Countering Anxious Themes

The trouble with anxious stories is that they restrict the freedom the child and the family have to work out new, creative solutions to current problems. They can also entrench problematic behavior into the serious patterns we call *pathology*. So, if the counselor identifies anxious stories, a goal for intervention is to reduce the problem focus on the child by offering the parents plausible new stories for explaining the current difficulties—themes that allow for more flexibility and nurturing rather than anxious involvement. To be therapeutic, the new story must reduce blaming and anxiousness in the family and refresh the parents' ability to see their child's behavior more objectively and respond to it appropriately.

The following section offers techniques counselors have used to both (1) inform parents, giving them new material for the stories they are composing about their child, and (2) reframe restrictive stories into more positive, flexible ones.

Looks Like Normal Development to Me

Instead of sticking exclusively to a problem focus, lay a background of "normative" talk. If you've seen the child or know the child, start off official meetings with a brief summary of the child's or teen's current social, emotional, and cognitive development. This conversation provides the parents with information about normal development, and this information from you often reduces their anxiety and broadens their understanding of their child. For example, understanding adolescents' needs to individuate helps parents reduce emotional reactivity when autonomy issues arise, increasing the odds that they will be able provide both warm support and firm limits for their offspring.

Use developmental concepts and language about normal transitions and adaptation to change. Sometimes parents gain a great deal of anxiety-reducing insight from discovering how their child's behavior might be a normal and healthy attempt to resolve conflicts or help the family get through a tough time.

When Mama Ain't Happy . . .

Sometimes, the counselor becomes convinced that the child's problem behavior is mirroring an aspect of adult relationships. If this is the case, brief marital counseling can be urged for the parents while supportive counseling for the child continues at school. Recently, for example, a 10-year-old girl began developing extreme and developmentally unusual separation anxiety following a family move. Her parents reasoned that the anxiety was a response to the move, but rather than resolving itself as the girl made new friends and did well at her new school, it increased. The counselor worked with the girl to help her recognize and cope with her anxious feelings. But a talk with the girl's mother also revealed that since the move, she had been feeling increasingly distressed by a growing emotional distance between herself and her husband. From a systems perspective, the daughter's increasing anxiety, manifesting itself in an inordinate need for closeness, paralleled the mother's increasing anxiety about the growing distance in her marriage. When marital issues were addressed through a referral to a community counselor, the daughter's behavior returned to normal.

You Don't Have to Be Perfect— In Fact, It Is Better If You Are Not

Psychoanalysts who study the effects of parent-child bonds in early life have concluded that the healthiest adults had something they call a *good-enough parent* while they were growing up. Apparently, when a parent is completely available and dependable, the child does not have an opportunity to develop important abilities such as delaying gratification, impulse control, and perspective-taking ability. Children need parents who are mostly responsive, predictable, and nurturing—in other words, "good enough," but also human.

Because children make mistakes, they must learn how to deal with themselves as imperfect people. The way parents treat their own mistakes, whether with denial or intolerance or compassion, offers children a model of how to deal with their own imperfections. Parents who accept their own mistakes with grace and a determination to learn from them give children an opportunity to learn a very valuable aspect of mental health. So, we can say to these perfectionist parents, it is good to fail now and then so your child can learn how to handle failure as well as success!

One parent educator, Michael Popkin, shared with me the Parent Affirmation of Imperfection (Figure 3.1). He uses this affirmation to keep parents focused on improvement, not perfection.

Sometimes Things Just Get Out of Sync

My favorite illustration for this comes from one mother who struggled to fit the parenting of two young adopted children into an already complex professional life. To her dismay, she could never seem to reach and stay at the point where she felt she had her life in control. She feared that either she or her children were defective! As a result of these feelings, she became more and more depressed about her own life, and more and more anxious about her own ability to parent. Fortunately, she reached out for help and came one time when we offered parenting classes. After recognizing her personal theme of underconfident apprehension, I offered her a more balanced and less anxious view of her children's development (and, therefore, herself). She eventually said,

> Oh, now I get it . . . as soon as you get the room all set up and working smoothly, they learn to crawl out of the crib. As soon as you get a bedtime routine working for one child, another outgrows the need for a nap. As soon as you have both of them in school, and you think things will finally settle into a routine, one

Accepting our own imperfection is vital to learning. The affirmation below is meant to help you focus on your goals and your strengths instead of your mistakes, clearing the way for excellence as a parent.

> *It's perfectly okay for me to be imperfect. This includes not being a perfect parent. This means that it's okay that I have already made a lot of mistakes as a parent and that it's okay that I will make other mistakes in the future. What's not okay is for me to pretend that I am perfect and to thereby hide my mistakes from myself. Instead, I will catch my mistakes with a smile rather than a kick and learn what they have to teach me. That way, I won't make the same mistakes too often, and I'll become a better and better parent. But I'll never be a perfect parent, and that's okay, because my goal is excellence, not perfection.*

How to use this affirmation:

Step 1: Read the affirmation through once.

Step 2: If you agree with what it says, read the affirmation through again, slowly. Relax and breathe deeply as you let the words sink deeper into your belief system.

Step 3: If you are having trouble, write the affirmation line by line on a blank sheet of paper. Pause after each line, and be aware of any thoughts or feelings that you have.

Step 4: If you are still having trouble forgiving yourself for your imperfections, repeat this affirmation daily until it feels comfortable for you.

Figure 3.1. The Parents' Affirmation of Imperfection
SOURCE: Popkin, 1987; used with permission.

of them joins a soccer team and your life is chaos again. And I guess it is always going to be this way: Since the children are always growing, the balance will always be changing.

She was right: Children change constantly and cycles of balancing and readjustment never end. Adopting this view helps parents stop blaming themselves and their children for the feeling that "things aren't working," and allows them to see that learning to do effective, efficient parenting is an ongoing process that requires constant readjustment, not an end point at which they should arrive.

A Good Fit Is Essential—
A Bad Fit Can Ruin Your Day (Week, Year)

The concept of a good fit takes the focus off of individual characteristics—such as the infamous suspected "bad genes"—and helps everyone focus on how various aspects of individuals fit together. This metaphor creates more "room" for everyone in the family to grow, because it acknowledges that we are all different, but we do best in situations that respect the characteristics and needs that we have. And we do poorly when we are forced to stay in situations that are a poor fit with our needs and interests.

For example, an adolescent whose needs are ignored in the school environment can develop symptoms that affect family functioning at home. Alternatively, sometimes the fit is bad between the needs a child has and the type of parenting in the home, and the child begins to act up or become depressed. Recently, a young adolescent was referred by his teachers because they were afraid he was becoming increasingly angry and depressed. When his parents were contacted, they said they were mystified about the concerns his teachers had expressed; in their view, he was doing fine and was a happy child. When the counselor got this boy to complete the life graph task (where children are asked to make a chart of their life, varying the height of the line depending on how good [high] or bad [low] they were feeling during each year of their life), he indicated that he was presently feeling so low he was off the charts. Clearly, there was a substantial lack of fit between this adolescent's perceptions of his life and his parents' perceptions of him, and this lack of fit probably was exacerbating his depression.

Counselors can help parents learn skills that enable them to provide parenting that better fits the needs of their child: sometimes more discipline and structure; sometimes more nurturing and warmth. Or they can help parents learn to treat a child with fitting, age-appropriate expectations for independence (instead of expectations that would better fit an older or younger child). Counselors can also help parents see that individual uniqueness is a valuable part of the interlocking family puzzle, rather than something that needs to be trimmed to fit.

That's Exactly What the Research Shows

This theme uses a counselor's expert power to counter parents' rigid, self-righteous themes ("No child of mine will ever act like that, have problems in school, etc."). One time-honored way in which to challenge rigidity is to cite experts who offer an alternative view. The benefit of this technique is that it is a quick way to counter child blaming; the counselor uses his or her influence to gain parental cooperation in viewing the child in a new way. I have used it to help parents understand the social changes associated with puberty timing ("Early-maturing girls often have these problems for a while, but they are often the best adjusted in later years," or "Late-maturing boys often feel like outsiders, but research shows they often develop an outstanding sense of humor and have happier relationships in midlife") and children's typical behavior changes in divorcing families ("This temporary drop in school grades is very common among children under similar circumstances"). Facts such as these, generated by experts, challenge restrictive and unhelpful views of the child's behavior. The goal is to provide parents with a way to understand the problem in a more comprehensive, less rigid manner. The use of this technique requires a counselor who is credible and comfortable with playing an expert role, however.

The Branch That Bends Survives the Storm

This is another theme that is useful in challenging rigid stories. Using techniques developed by rational-emotive therapy, the counselor coaches the parent to examine rigid story lines rationally and generate new ones that are more realistic or helpful. Sometimes, the parent needs to know, one has to "give" a little.

One parent recently blamed her daughter's problem on the fact that "she is running around with all these other kids at school who are not like *us,* and no daughter of mine . . ." This rigid stand was creating a great deal of tension between mother and daughter, with the daughter deliberately provoking her mother by bringing home every peer she could who was "not like us." As the counselor helped the mother stop and examine what she really wanted for her daughter's social development, the mother developed more rational expectations for her daughter's behavior. Eventually, she changed her rigid edict from "No daughter of mine . . ." to "I want my daughter to choose healthy friends." As the mother's rigidity on this issue diminished, the daughter began genuinely exploring her own friendship needs and preferences instead of choosing friends for their shock value.

Extended Family Members Raising Kids

Before concluding this chapter, let's turn to the group of families where the adults are often the most anxious and the children are sometimes the most troubled. These are the families where grandparents, aunt, uncles, family friends, or older siblings are raising a child because the child's own biological parents cannot or will not. Typically, this is because some crisis has occurred—perhaps the parents have deserted the child, or have gone to prison, or are disabled or deceased. Or perhaps they have been judged by the courts as not being able to care for their own children. In any case, these children and their families are among the most stressed of all we serve.

This is not to say that children whose caregivers are not their biological parents have the most problems, or that nonbiological caregivers face insurmountable challenges. On the contrary, every counselor can think of healthy, well-balanced children who are popular, make good grades, and get elected to student council while being raised by nonparental adults. Nevertheless, these families are often desperate for some reassurance and assistance. Aware of the deep needs (and past traumas) of the child they are raising, and aware of their own possible deficiencies, these adults are usually quite responsive to a counselor's efforts to provide family support. They often feel "rusty" about child development and discipline techniques, so they are primed for just the kind of information we can give. In addition, these families get a great deal out of knowing each other. They feel encouraged when they discover that they are not the only ones who have taken on this challenge,

In other words, these families are often well served by structured group programs and workshops, where they can get both information and social support. The remaining chapters discuss the "how to" of offering structured group programs for parents and other caregivers.

4

Inviting Parents to Become Involved

The results of hundreds of studies are clear: There are many benefits from schools and families having a close working relationship. Nearly every school has, by now, developed some kind of plan for involving parents, at least on paper. More often than not, the school counselor is given sole or partial responsibility for implementing the plan.

There are differences in philosophies of parent involvement, and these differences lead to different goals and different strategies for achieving these goals. Currently, there seem to be three distinct philosophies of the ideal relationship between parents and caregivers and the schools. The most common of these is *task orientation*. This is the most traditional view; in this orientation, faculty, staff, and administration work to involve the parents as tutors, aides, attendance monitors, fund raisers, field trip monitors, band boosters, and clerical help. Sometimes parents are asked to help with problem areas such as being sure that homework is done or school behavior is corrected. The task orientation seems to be the type of home-school relationship preferred by many teachers and administrators.

In *process orientation*, parents are asked to participate in activities that are important to the educational process. These activities may include curriculum planning, textbook review and selection, membership on task forces and committees, teacher review and selection, and helping to set dress codes and behavior standards. A process orientation is not widespread because school professionals often do not feel comfortable sharing these responsibilities with parents. Nevertheless, it is a growing trend. A process orientation promotes a strong sense of ownership among parents for their child's educational experiences, and these feelings of ownership seem to help parents insist on children's regular school attendance, responsible academic effort, and staying in school.

A *developmental orientation* helps parents and caregivers develop skills that will benefit themselves, their children, the school, the teachers, and the families at the same time. This type of orientation is exemplified in community schools and Head Start programs. Parents give time, energy, or resources to school in ways that capitalize on their strengths. At the same time, they are given opportunities to learn about the development of their child and about parenting practices that both nurture children and provide structure for their lives. They also may be offered opportunities to learn vocational and life skills.

Ideally, comprehensive home-school partnerships can accommodate all three orientations. Parents help with specific tasks, develop skills that will benefit themselves and their child, and shape the educational experience for all children in their community. The most successful parent programs are those where the majority of parents feel empowered by making contributions to the school and have a sense of ownership in the planning and execution of the school's programs. Under these circumstances, schools have the most beneficial effects on the lives of children, their families, and their communities.

1. Recognize, listen to, and accept the concerns and expectations of each parent.

2. Identify goals that are agreed on by both the parents and the school staff persons with whom work will be done.

3. Offer clear instructions about the options available to parents during the decision-making process.

4. Show genuine commitment, patience, perseverance, and a good sense of humor.

5. Encourage an atmosphere of mutual cooperation and interdependence; model good teamwork.

6. Provide times and location where parents can meet and visit with each other and school staff.

7. Be gracious and respectful in inviting parents into the school; express genuine gratitude for any time or effort that they give.

Figure 4.1. Guidelines for Involving Parents in the Schools

Figure 4.1 provides some guidelines that apply to all three types of orientations for working effectively with parents.

Developing a Comprehensive Home-School Partnership

One pragmatic school counselor, when asked about her philosophy of parent involvement, laughed, "I'll take them any way I can get them!" This wise counselor offers parents a range of options for becoming involved at school, from occasionally joining her and the child for lunch to volunteering in the school on a daily basis. She believes that parents need to be able to "plug in" at any level they feel good about, and even a little involvement is better than none. "A small thing has a good chance of growing into something more parents begin to feel like they belong to," she says.

Many parents are not able to come to school during workday hours, but there are still opportunities to be involved. Following are a few ways counselors have found to keep the door open.

Schoolwide Activities

- Mini-workshops introduce parents to the school's policies, procedures, and programs. (Some studies show that this is what parents want more than anything else.)
- Family nights, cultural dinners, carnivals, and potluck dinners bring people together in a nonthreatening way.
- Fairs and bazaars involve parents in fund-raising and teamwork.
- Performances and plays in which a child has a part often bring the child's family to school.

Communication Activities

- Telephone hotlines: Parents can take turns staffing these to give information about special events coming up, communicable diseases, or other information.
- Newsletters: Often a parent is willing to help produce these, and they are an excellent way of keeping other parents informed of special events and classroom projects, materials needs, and the like.

Service Activities

- Help the parents establish a lending library of their favorite parenting books. Ask for donations from local bookstores.
- Child care: Some parents won't come to conferences or programs because they care for many children and can't make arrangements to get away without them. Other parents may be glad to help with arrangements so all families can participate.
- Parent support groups: Many parents report that they benefit a great deal simply by getting to know other families so they

can be supportive of each other. (More about this option in Chapter 5.)

Decision Activities

- Ask for parent involvement in curriculum planning. When parents know about the curriculum, they are more supportive of it at home.

- Ask for parent involvement with other school needs. Some schools have no way to enhance the playground, paint the lunchroom, or landscape the grounds unless parents are involved. When parents know they are genuinely needed and the invitation to be involved is real, not for show, they can get together and do amazing things!

Rather than requiring a great deal of leadership from the counselor, getting parents involved is often simply a matter of not getting in the way—and remembering to demonstrate genuine appreciation for parents' ideas and efforts.

For example, one mother decided when her son was a fifth grader that she was tired of hearing him complain about the lunchroom. He had complained about the food, the staff who policed the children's behavior, the noise, and the ugly outgrown cafeteria every day for 5 years! This parent was convinced that impoverished environments (such as the cafeteria) promote children's misbehavior. So she rounded up the parents of his classmates and they embarked on a yearlong project to "humanize" the cafeteria. With the help of the art teacher, children produced fabric art; parents made these into brightly colored quilts and hung them from the ceiling. Other parents hand-painted the walls of the cafeteria, and one classroom of kids spatter-painted the worn-looking lockers that lined one wall. As a result of these changes, children had a "new" lunchroom with a friendly, inviting, child-friendly atmosphere; parents had a place in the school that had been created by their own efforts and of which they felt proud. The children also had a daily reminder that parents cared enough to get involved at school.

What did these improvements cost the school personnel? Very little. The parents initially worked with the school counselor to present their idea; he encouraged them and arranged meetings with the school principal. The counselor and the principal unlocked the building so parents could work after hours, they each dropped in now and then and smiled encouragingly at the parents wielding paint-brushes and ladders. The counselor also coordinated with the teachers to plan a thank-you party for the parents when the work was done. The whole project was an example of how empowering parents to become involved in ways that are meaningful to them requires a little up-front effort, but produces rewards that are beyond what anyone might have first imagined.

Sometimes schools and communities decide to commit effort to an outreach program that has a particular intervention focus. For example, some schools with many children at risk for dropping out seek to join forces with parents to promote student academic success from both fronts. Other communities have decided that helping students find a place in the world of work (instead of the world of welfare) is a goal best achieved by getting families and schools together to do career exploration. Still others are innovating with ways to prevent child abuse by enhancing the parent-child relationship. The following section offers an overview of some of the creative alternatives for home-school partnership programs being developed. Resources for obtaining more information on these programs are included in the Resources and References sections at the end of this book.

Promoting Student Academic Success

Decades of research have consistently found that children with high achievement scores have parents who have high expectations for them, who respond to and interact with them frequently, and who see themselves as teachers of their own children. Parent education programs that focus on children's academic success foster these success-promoting attitudes and skills. As parents become more effective, their children increase in language skills, perform better on tests, and behave in more socially appropriate ways at school. Parent education programs that promote student academic success seem to be especially helpful to low-income or other at-risk families. The sooner parents develop these skills, the better, so targeting families with young children obtains the greatest benefit.

Several programs of this sort are available. Some publishers have developed videotape programs that are either checked out and taken home by parents or used to foster discussion in group sessions. Examples of these include *Parents on Board* and *Smart Start for Parents*. Also in this category are the growing number of family literacy programs that seek to involve parents and children together in developing reading skills and enjoying literature.

Promoting Student Vocational Success

A recent innovation in parent education, and one that targets the parents of middle or high school students, is focused on promoting vocational success. Most schools sponsor a career fair for students and parents, and perhaps a college application information session. These efforts are ineffective in reaching many students and their parents, however.

Observing the pitfalls often encountered by students from first- or second-generation families or historically oppressed groups (Figure 4.2), counselors in New York developed the Career Awareness Program for Chinese and Korean American parents. Counselors saw that the adolescents from these families had difficulty when encouraged to do career exploration; soon they learned that many families of these teens regarded it as their responsibility to choose a career path for the child. Therefore, attempts to encourage the adolescents' independent career exploration were more than futile! Parents were invited to attend 10 separate workshops on evenings and weekends. The workshops incorporated discussions on decision-making strategies, resources available to immigrant families to promote their children's education, and facts about particular areas of employment. The program helped eliminate the obstacles to career exploration experienced by many first- or second-generation immigrant children.

- The family sees time to study, a place to study, freedom from household or financial burdens as special (and unfair) privileges.
- The family insists that the student pick one career path and stick with it early on.
- The family picks the career for the student, without realizing that other career paths could also be equally (or more) stable, lucrative, respectable, or rewarding.
- The family may discourage the student from pursuing an appropriate career path because of mistaken beliefs about the demands, educational requirements, or acculturation pressures of that occupation.
- The family is not emotionally supportive of the student's vocational interests, usually because of fears of losing family closeness and the dissipation of traditional family values.

Figure 4.2. Potential Family Obstacles to Career Exploration and Development

Another counselor who worked primarily with Haitian families borrowed the family therapy technique of constructing genograms (a multigenerational graphic representation of a person's family of origin) and adapted it to gathering career information (Figure 4.3). When the counselor worked with teens and their parents over several weeks to gather information about the meaning of work and kinds of work families had engaged in through the generations, a good foundation was laid for the students' current career explorations.

Career genograms are a way for students to show respect for their family's history and culture and find a way to connect that to the decisions they will make in the contemporary world of work. In general, career development programs that involve the parents allow students to reconcile messages about work from home, school, and the dominant culture, allowing them to make the choices that are best for them.

- ▨ Explain to the student (and parent) what a genogram is and why you are going to use it.
- ▨ Maintain an atmosphere of partnership and openness; keep the chart you are constructing out in the middle of you.
- ▨ Use the verbatim information the family offers to fill in the chart; for example, if you hear that great-grandmother was a *curandera*, write that down. (If a translation is also offered, include it in parentheses.)
- ▨ Ask questions such as, What did your (mother/father/ aunt/uncle, etc.) do for a living? What do you remember about their jobs/career? How long did your (relative) go to school? Did your (relative) ever dream of doing something else?
- ▨ When the basic information is recorded, look for family occupational patterns, individual "exceptions" to the family tradition, socioeconomic patterns, gender-related patterns, etc.
- ▨ Stay attuned to the nonverbal behavior of the teen (and/or parents) as this information is shared and discussed; use it for suggesting interpretations, directions for further exploration, etc.

Figure 4.3. Techniques for Constructing Family Career Genograms

Promoting Parenting Skills and Family Emotional Health

A number of programs to develop parenting skills have been developed in recent years, including Active Parenting, Parent Effectiveness Training (PET), and Systematic Training for Effective Parenting (STEP). Most school counselors find that these programs are very successful, especially when parents feel the need for them (and are therefore invested in them) and when a dynamic facilitator provides the right mix of support and challenge. A family involvement coordinator for one school related this story:

One single mother of three attended one of my Active Parenting workshops because she had lost custody of one of her children and was really having a hard time. After the program, she pulled her life back together and was able to get her child back. She still drops by regularly for a hug and to let me know how she is doing. She said that whenever she is struggling with her children, she looks back at her Parents Workbook and flips through the other handouts. She say it is what keeps her going on the right track.

Feedback like this proves how valuable this option is for many families.

Some school counselors are experimenting with another in vivo approach to learning ways to interact more effectively with children. *Filial therapy*, as it has been called, is a method of training parents to respond and interact therapeutically with their children by enhancing the parent-child relationship. Developed by Louise and Bernard Guerney (1989) and refined by Garry Landreth (1991; Kraft & Landreth, 1998) at the University of North Texas, filial therapy takes place in a support group format, where parents learn basic child-centered play therapy principles to use with their children in special weekly play sessions. Over 6 to 8 weeks, parents are given information and feedback on their behavior with their child during the play sessions. (Sometimes parents videotape these; sometimes they practice a play session with the group watching in the background.) With this support, parents become more effective at accurately tracking the child's language and behavior, acknowledging and reflecting the child's emotions without judgment, and setting limits on the child's behavior, when necessary, in a firm but supportive way.

The filial therapy model has been used and shown to be effective with a wide range of parents, from middle-class suburban mothers to incarcerated fathers. It may be especially helpful for preventing problems in families that are at risk for child abuse, because it

- increases parents' empathic behaviors toward their children;
- increases parents' acceptance of their children; and
- reduces parenting stress.

"Sometimes it helps to have a special time and place to play."

Definition[a]

Filial therapy is a specific, limited time of interaction between a parent and child during which selected play materials and parent responses facilitate the development of a safe time for the child to express and explore self fully (feelings, thoughts, experiences, and behaviors) through the child's natural medium of communication: play.

Rationales for Filial Therapy[b]

Play is the natural medium of expression for children.

Play bridges the gap between concrete experience and abstract thought.

Play is children's attempt to organize their experience.

Children gain a sense of control through play.

Through play, children learn coping skills.

Filial therapy promotes a parent's deeper understanding of the child.

Filial therapy allows the child to be more expressive with the parent.

Behavioral and emotional control learned in playtimes generalize to other occasions.

Basic Principles of Filial Therapy[c]

During play therapy time, the parent

- is warm and friendly with the child;
- accepts the child exactly as he or she is;
- establishes a feeling of permissiveness ("During this time, you decide . . . ");
- recognizes and reflects feelings expressed by the child to help the child gain insight into his or her behavior;

Figure 4.4. Filial Therapy Essentials

a. Adapted from Landreth (1991).
b. Adapted from Landreth (1991).
c. Landreth, (1991), pp. 77-78.

- respects the child's ability to solve his or her own problems;
- does not direct;
- does not attempt to hurry "therapeutic" processes; and
- establishes only necessary limits.

Therapeutic Parent Responses in Filial Therapy[d]

Empathic Responding

To feelings: "It really hurts when your friends won't help you."

To thoughts: "You think that's for little kids."

To action (tracking): "You're going to put it in the trash can."

Purpose of tracking—To convey the following messages:

1. I hear.
2. I see.
3. I'm here.
4. I care.
5. I understand.

Characteristics of Therapeutic Responses

1. Short and interactive
2. Return responsibility to the child
3. Touch on feelings whenever possible
4. Provide freedom to be creative
5. Focus on the child
6. Give recognition (effort) and not evaluation (product)

Limit Setting[e]

Purpose

1. Provide security, prevent future guilt feelings. (Not hurt self, others, property)
2. Provide opportunity for child to practice self-control
3. Anchor the child's experience to reality

Figure 4.4. Filial Therapy Essentials *(continued)*

d. Landreth (1991), Chapter 10, pp. 183-208.
e. Landreth (1991), pp. 222-223.

(continued)

Three Steps to Limit Setting

1. Acknowledge the child's feeling, wants
2. Communicate the limit
3. Target an alternative

Materials[f]

Include real-life toys, acting-out or aggression-release toys, and toys for creative expression and emotional release. Keep the filial therapy toys separate. Include such things as house, mom-dad-children figures, first-aid kit, small plastic figures of dinosaurs, cops and robbers, jungle animals, play dough, scissors, tape, crayons, paper, rubber knife, puppets (at least one mean-looking one), car, cash register, play money, and rope.

Figure 4.4. Filial Therapy Essentials *(continued)*
f. Landreth (1991).

The challenge in the school setting is finding a time and place to conduct these groups. Writing a grant to help garner support for such a program can be done, however, and funding agencies are particularly interested in innovative programs that prevent later problems in at-risk groups. For an outline of information provided to parents during the sessions, see Figure 4.4.

Emotion coaching is another parent support/psychoeducational program that targets the emotional climate between parents and children. Developed by John Gottman (Gottman, Katz, & Hooven, 1996) and adapted by others, emotion coaching is a parent education program that specifically promotes healthier interactions by teaching parents to move away from being *emotion dismissing* with their children and toward being *emotion coaching* parents—in other words, parents who fully acknowledge their children's emotions and help them learn what to do with them.

Counselors in our community offered this parent program to parents who were involved in separation or divorce, thinking that this transition point might be a key time to foster changes in parenting behavior. The workshop was enormously popular with this group of emotionally stressed parents. They reported that it not only helped them deal with their children's emotions during this difficult time, but helped them deal more effectively with their own emotions as well. An outline for conducting emotion coaching sessions with parents is presented in Figure 4.5.

Promoting Parent Development and Family Empowerment

Parent empowerment programs are seen by some as the wave of the future. These programs are firmly grounded in the philosophy that in a democratic society, the public schools belong to the parents and citizens of a community. From this perspective, school professionals are actually public servants who are entrusted to use their expertise to help create the best school system possible. The schools don't belong to the professionals—the teachers, counselors, and administrators—but to the community, and we use our knowledge and skills to help the community build effective schools. According to this view, parents aren't needed to supplement or support the agenda of the professional. Instead, parents are told that they must be involved because the schools belong to them. In diverse communities, parent involvement is especially desirable as a way to ensure that no one particular group dominates the decision-making processes for the schools.

These kinds of programs are based on the time-honored notion of teaching parents to fish for themselves rather than catching them fish for a day. Counselors make their expertise in group process available and their resources for contacting families accessible, but they communicate to parents that the ultimate goal is for the parents to guide, lead, and support themselves. Counselors get parents together to talk about concerns they have, needs they have, and changes they'd like to see in the schools. Then, counselors teach parents the knowledge and skills they need to be influential in a large system such as a school district.

Goal: To help parents move away from being emotion dismissing adults and toward being emotion coaching adults

Week 1

1. Introductions; ice breaker.
2. Explain plan for the coming weeks: how many, what times, etc.; ground rules (mutual support, group confidentiality, etc.).
3. Explain the emotion coaching curriculum.
   a. Goal of emotion coaching
   b. Importance of emotion coaching
      i. When one adult in a child's life can help a child learn what to do with and how to talk about his or her emotions, this tends to counter other effects of family stress that we commonly see, such as lower grades, withdrawal from or trouble getting along with peers, trouble getting along with teachers or other authority figures, being sick more often, acting out or withdrawal at home, and lower self-esteem.
      ii. Emotion coaching teaches a child skills that help relationships: the relationship with oneself (more accepting of self means higher self-esteem) and relationships with others (children understand how to share their emotions with others in a constructive way and understand others' emotions better, do not become as frightened when Mom or Dad or other adults are upset, and do not assume these emotions are their own fault).
4. Understanding our own emotional history.
   a. Think about, then discuss, how emotions were dealt with in our own growing-up years.
      i. On an index card, answer the following questions:

      When you were mad, whom could you go to? Not go to?
      When you were sad, whom could you go to? Not go to?
      When you were frightened, whom could you go to? Not go to?
      When you were happy, whom could you go to? Not go to?
      ii. Look for patterns and share these with the group.

Figure 4.5. Emotion Coaching: A Psychoeducational Group for Parents

    b. How people were with us affects how comfortable we are with our own children's emotions. Imagine one of your children before you, being mad, sad, frightened, or happy. Now reflect; which of these emotions in your child are you most comfortable with? Least? Discuss.

5. Homework: During the week that follows, collect an example of your child *being angry*. Do not try to change anything about how it usually goes, just be a human video camera and try to notice everything: your child's facial expressions, body, voice, actions, words. Remember everything as clearly as you can. We will anonymously share these examples next week.

6. Close.

Week 2

1. Introduce new members, review names, review ground rules.
2. Review goal of emotion coaching (see handout).
3. Introduce more detail about how emotion coaching benefits children.

("As you left last week, you may have wondered, now what exactly am I going to learn? And how is it going to benefit my children?") Explain illustration of the brain. Simply: lower brain, mid-brain, higher brain.

    a. The origin of emotions is in the very basic, primitive part of our brains. This part of us we share with animals— think of a dog you know snarling in anger, trembling in fear, acting sad and lifeless, content and happy.

    Emotions: Instantaneous and reactive. Useful for survival. Example: Hitting someone back who has hit you, reflexively.

    b. Our midbrain is more like what we have in common with clever monkeys. The basic emotions are still triggered, but there is also a primitive ability to *use* them in a way that helps us meet a goal. For example, pretending not to be scared. Pretending to be happy or mad.

Figure 4.5. Emotion Coaching: A Psychoeducational Group for Parents *(continued)*

Emotions: May be repressed (stuffing tissues back in the box). Results in physiological changes that affect mental processing and physical well-being. Also may be useful for survival. Example: A child hiding her anger in order not to provoke parent into hitting her. Result: Child gets very confused about what she, herself, really feels.

c. Our higher brain is the cerebral cortex; it is what makes us special and unique as human beings. The cerebral cortex is advanced enough to use language. Emotions can be put into words, which we use to talk to ourselves or with others. Putting emotions into words, reasoning about them, and making decisions about how to express them helps the body get back to a more relaxed state (which promotes health). It also frees up more brain space for cognitive processing and memory.

Emotions: Are noticed, felt, and labeled. May be shared with other people. Self-talk may be used to soothe one's self. The emotion is accepted for what it is, and often deliberate choices are made about how to express the feeling further. The feelings often lead to plans for the future, that is, "Next time I start feeling scared, I'm going to . . . "

Questions?

4. How do parents help children use their higher brain more than their lower or middle brain when they are emotional?

a. Emotion coaching, not emotion dismissing.

i. Emotion coaching—think of Mr. Rogers. All emotions are OK, they are simply your emotions. They don't make you bad or good. They don't mean you are dangerous or weak. They are just feelings, which every human has.

Helps child label the feeling.
Gives child permission to really feel the feeling.
Stays with child while he or she has the feeling.
Helps child talk about the feeling.
May help child create plans for the future. ("What else could you do?")

Figure 4.5. Emotion Coaching: A Psychoeducational Group for Parents *(continued)*

Result: Child learns to do this for self!

   ii. Emotion dismissing involves some combination of these:

Ignores child's emotions.

Tells child to "get over it."

Shames child for having the emotion.

Abandons child when emotions are strong ("When you can pull yourself together and stop this crying, I'll talk to you.").

Acts indifferent to the child's experience.

Result: Child gets out of touch with self, while still experiencing the effects of the emotion.

   iii. Role-play the difference.

5. Break into groups small enough for discussion and more role-play.
   a. Write down on card the basics of a recent "mad" situation with your child.
   b. Shuffle cards. In pairs, role-play the situations in pairs. The rest of the group critiques and provides suggestions for improvement in the role—trying to get examples where parent is very dismissing and very "coaching."
6. Close

Subsequent Weeks: Follow same basic outline as week 2, focusing on a different emotion. For example, mad, sad, glad/happy, fearful/anxious, or something else the group picks.

Figure 4.5. Emotion Coaching: A Psychoeducational Group for Parents *(continued)*
SOURCE: Adapted from workshops presented by John Gottman.

In one such program, the parents at an at-risk urban school recently decided to work on two issues. Because they were concerned about the number of kids hanging around after school with nothing to do, they wanted a regular, structured, after-school tutoring program that they could count on, and they wanted some after-school sports opportunities available for kids who weren't necessarily involved on official school sports teams. The counselors saw their role as change agents who could teach the parents democratic process skills of how to be heard and work for change in the system. Being successful in influencing the school system helped these marginalized parents feel more invested in their schools and their community. They were encouraged to participate more in shaping the direction of the lives of their children. As a result, change was made in the schools, but the children also benefited by having involved parents.

Other examples of parent empowerment programs such as these include MALDEF's Parent Leadership Program with the Los Angeles Unified School District and the PEP-Si' (Parent Empowerment Program-Students Included/Padres en Poder-Si') in Santa Barbara, California. MALDEF's goal is educational equity for the Hispanic community; the foundational belief is that parent involvement in the governance and decision-making process of the school is an essential factor in improving educational opportunities for Hispanic children. To promote this goal, 12 2-hour classes meet weekly, at two different times of day and days of the week, to accommodate the work schedules of parents. The major focus of the classes includes information about how the school functions, experiential sessions on conducting parent-teacher conferences, dialogues with community leaders, meetings with school officials, and the development of a team project.

PEP-Si' targeted families with students in the transition from elementary to junior high school and included multiple components that were all coordinated by each school's counselor. These multiple components included a student development component, a parent outreach component, a tutorial component, and a community component (that involved obtaining support from local businesses). The outcome of this broad-based program was very positive from the perspective of both the students and their parents.

Even with programs like these, however, the burden of effort rests on the counselor until the school officials and the parents catch the vision of the parents organizing and running the parent involvement activities themselves. Certainly, this is possible—parents everywhere get involved in other organizations on behalf of their children, without the benefit of government-sponsored staff, and run these organizations quite effectively for themselves. Perhaps the challenges we face in the new century will foster the ideal: more parent involvement programs that are "of the parents, by the parents, and for the parents."

Meanwhile, some parents have only enough energy to show up at school when programs are offered, but not enough to provide leadership in a grassroots effort to affect school governance. For these parents, the opportunity to take advantage of developmental programs sponsored by a trusted school counselor is a boon to a busy life. "At the end of my day, I'm really thankful to have the chance to sit and watch somebody else run the show," one single mother once said. "I learn a lot, and I enjoy being in adult company." In the next chapter, I shall look at ways to make these school-sponsored programs as beneficial for parents as possible.

5

Tips From the Trenches

CREATING SUCCESSFUL PROGRAMS FOR PARENTS

A good rule of thumb for busy counselors who want to create more interaction with parents is the adage "why reinvent the wheel?" Indeed, if there are other good wheels around that seem to work well in your kind of terrain, then imitate them!

There is, however, no one-size-fits-all solution when it comes to either wheels or programs for involving parents. Schools are unique, and so are the counselors who serve them. Communities are unique, and so are the families within them. Therefore, there is no one plan for success that can be adopted by all. Occasionally, though, we fall prey to our wishful thinking that somebody else has a quick and easy solution that we can just borrow and implement and get the same successful results.

This recently happened in one state where, in response to a local crisis of violence, an entire community came together in the schools, shared its concerns and vision, and mobilized itself to become actively involved. Some farsighted counselors caught the wave of interest and developed a grassroots program to train parent facilitators; they also published a resource guide full of information that could be shared on basic child development, family communication, easing school transitions, and effective discipline. Impressed with the stunning success of this program in one community, state officials adopted the model and spent a great deal of money training staff and parent liaisons to implement the program in every district across the state. To everyone's surprise, the program that had been so successful in one area created barely a ruffle of interest in parents elsewhere.

Rather than becoming bitter when our best-laid plans produce disappointing results, we can remind ourselves that there is no one blueprint for success that can be adopted by all. Even if we hit on something successful this year, there is no one plan that will work forever. What we can do, however, is continue to share ideas with each other, try them out, use the ones that work, and let the others go.

In this spirit, what follows is a collection of favorite tips. Many of these ideas were shared by parenting professionals at Leader Training Workshops offered by Active Parenting Publishers. The ideas are grouped into categories that might be helpful to think about, from when you first are considering a new parent program to wrapping it up and evaluating your efforts.

Know Your Parents

Chapter 1 offers several ways for thinking about the current physical, emotional, psychological, and social needs of the adults you want to reach. Be sure you have them firmly in mind as you begin to plan so that you can reach parents where they're at.

Consider Your Community

Learn the youth-serving systems and community resources in place to serve families and how to make them work. If you need to, can you help a family get past local "gatekeepers" and get results?

Strengthen your community network ties so you can keep your finger on the pulse of the concrete needs and challenges of families in your locale. These change! For several years, our community offered a workshop for both adults and children of families going through a divorce. It was very popular; we had families on the waiting list to take it. Then suddenly there seemed to be no interest. Asking around, we found that similar workshops were now being offered by many local churches. We decided we would do better shifting our attention and efforts to offering something else.

Plan Your Program

Get Help

Find a volunteer to assist with coordination efforts—child care, carpooling, equipment, snacks, and publicity. The PTA or another school club in the district may be a good source of volunteers. Another source of volunteer helpers is graduate child development majors or counseling, psychology, family therapy, and social work trainees who need experience hours.

Consider Child Care

Use careful consideration when attempting this. Voluntary child care is popular because it involves no cost to parents, but if you choose it, be aware of quality issues. Child care providers should be committed to the same philosophy of discipline and communication that you are trying to get across to the parents.

You will need a child-friendly site. The person coordinating child care should know the expectations for the room; for example, should toys be put back exactly where they were taken from? Are some toys or games off limits?

Snacks add to the ambiance, but if you do offer them, check with parents about whether they want snacks for their child. It is even more important to plan to keep kids busy—they need some structured time as well as free-choice time, and it is great to have someone who can help with homework.

Sponsorship and Donations

Ask churches, the chamber of commerce, the YMCA or YWCA, and other interest groups if they will help get the word out or be willing to cosponsor a program with you. Attend civic group luncheons and ask to give a brief mini-presentation; make your presentation lively with video clips, a flip chart, colorful handouts, and lots of time for questions and answers.

Can someone sponsor bus passes or taxi coupons so transportation issues will be easier? Ask for coffee and day-old bakery donations from local grocery stores or restaurants. Find a group that will sponsor scholarships for the children of participants in your program to attend other community events such as the county fair or a concert.

Scheduling

Look at the community schedule and offer sessions at a time that will least interfere with youth sports programs and holiday plans. Early fall and early spring or late winter work well for many. Some have found Friday evening is popular with working parents. (Although it takes a very special breed of counselor to opt for this plan!) For parents without jobs, having classes at school while kids are already there is most convenient. In other communities, offering a lunchtime series at the workplace (when there are only a few major employers) gets good results.

Site

Many parents find comfort in the fact that the school is sponsoring the program. Alternatively, use a site such as a library, hospital, or other community center where parents currently attend other workshops. Sometimes it helps to have the site near a bus line.

Get Parents to Come

Be sure your program is in the school newsletter and announced at the PTA meetings. Better yet, offer to do a mini-presentation at PTA or other group meetings so parents can meet you and sense your enthusiasm and experience your style. Ask other guidance counselors to mention your program to specific parents whom they believe would benefit from it. Invite teachers to attend; if they are familiar with your program, they are more likely to help you involve the parents with whom they have contact. Ask friends and family to talk it up.

Some counselors have had good luck with mailing personal letters of invitation to families they especially want to come. Other counselors find that nothing beats good old one-on-one personal contact.

Local radio stations often have a weekly slot for interviews on a talk show where people can call in with questions. Try to get on one! This gives you a chance to talk about the content or philosophy of your program. Newspapers sometimes do public service announcements or will add you to the community calendar. Don't forget the neighborhood association calendar or newsletter.

Offer meals or at least refreshments. For people of many backgrounds and traditions, offering food is essential for establishing a true sense of community. Once you've begun, you might want to trade around this responsibility—it adds to parents' sense of contributing to the group.

Be a Charismatic Leader

Knowledgeable, spirited, and caring facilitators are the key to a successful program. Be enthusiastic! Energy is contagious. Talk to parents directly and share your personal reasons for being excited about the program.

Consider getting a coleader who is the opposite gender from you, so both genders of parents have someone they can identify with. In some cases, it is also good to have coleaders who are from different racial or ethnic groups. This may help some parents feel more comfortable. Leaders who respectfully bridge differences in their own backgrounds are living examples of how this can be done.

Remember, you will encounter all kinds of families. You must not portray yourself as a leader who has all the answers. Instead, you have a unique opportunity to learn from these parents and to create a climate where they can learn from each other.

Build rapport and trust every chance you get. Your ability to communicate and form relationships with the families who come allows you to lead them beyond their limitations and dysfunctions. Even when parents become very discouraged about their children, your attitude must remain helpful and enthusiastic. Don't give up!

Allow yourself to draw energy from certain participants who are responding well to your efforts. Use this positive energy to balance the discouragement you may feel from parents who are flat-faced, unenthusiastic, or challenge you. Don't get discouraged. Often the parents who are at first the most reluctant and resistant are later the most enthusiastic.

If a crisis develops in the group, gently take charge. Your experience and training are your greatest strengths when you find yourself with heated emotions and confusion. Stay cool. Acknowledge the difficulty, but lead the group back to a constructive task.

Once when I was finishing up a group session, asking for questions or comments, a woman across the room stood up and dramatically said, "I just want you to know that I have sat here and listened to this whole thing and I think everything you've said is worthless!" Of course my heart rate doubled with this kind of surprise attack, but I found a way to acknowledge her disappointment, and offered to hear more after the whole group was dismissed. She didn't stick around to take me up on my offer, but many other parents whispered thanks and encouragement to me that night as their way of making up for her. The trade-off was almost worth it! Others later said, "I learned a lot from how you handled her." Parents appreciate a calm, warm, and confident leadership style.

Motivate and Encourage

Be available to welcome and chat with early arrivals. Do all setup tasks well in advance so you can greet people personally as they come in. Do all cleanup tasks after they leave and position yourself by the door so you can smile good-bye to each person. Think airlines! The men and women who fly the friendly skies know what it takes to keep you coming back. Borrow ideas from them. Your friendly, positive attitude will help parents feel better when they leave than when they arrived. This helps them know that their time and efforts are worth it.

Have parents set goals in the beginning—and go back to them several times. People need to see that they are making progress; this enhances internal motivation. Work with parents to come up with a workable plan for success with their child. Borrow ideas from brief solution-focused counseling to encourage parents to look for small improvements that occur as they progress from week to week. When parents begin to feel overwhelmed, exude confidence that there is light at the end of the tunnel—and it is not a train!

Treat parents like professionals. Prepare registration lists or sign-in books; have parents check themselves off as they arrive. Be sure people have name tags. If parents are attending a workshop, prepare folders for them with the name of the workshop, session dates and times, facilitator name and phone number, a sharpened pencil, and a donated notepad.

Make sure parents have time to connect personally with each other—"buddy time," as some group leaders call it. You might want to ask parents to pick buddy pairs the first night and give them the job of keeping their buddy encouraged. This helps promote a feeling of belonging for the participants—very important for the success of your program, but important for the lasting effects beyond your program too.

Some schools are able to offer weekly cash door prizes (supplied by the PTA or other donor), food baskets, or other incentives for parent participants. A reward system like this can add to the sense of fun; who doesn't like the feeling of winning the lottery?

Take a few minutes to phone no-shows during the week, expressing concern. "I knew you said you'd all been sick a lot lately, so I thought I'd check and see if you were doing OK." Parents really appreciate this kind of personal attention! They know it means a lot for you to take time to contact them individually. Or you might phone some of those who attended to hear how they are doing with their new skills. Or send out note cards offering encouragement. Such ongoing contact helps parents stay involved in the program.

When you are offering parents new skills, remember the comments they make and use their names in examples. Bring up what they've shared before as a great example of the current topic, so they realize that you remember and appreciate their contributions to the group.

When ending a session, briefly discuss topics to be included at the next session to build interest. Emphasize that some of next week's topics could make a real difference in the family's well-being.

Appeal to the enlightened self-interest of people to get them involved in any endeavor. Use their contributions to develop a program that serves and empowers! A packet of fancy brochures does not help a family or child in crisis. Instead, they need hope, practical information, and new skills.

Have a Great First Meeting

The first meeting can make or break a group's commitment, so it is worth it to spend extra effort on the front end. Find a volunteer to call everyone before the first meeting to welcome them and remind them about the time, place, and agenda. Find some other volunteers (perhaps a school club?) to make a colorful "Welcome!" poster. Have coffee or some other beverage available. Think of any way you can to help the group feel comfortable and not threatened.

Sometimes it is nice to assemble a resource table of children's books, parents' books, videos, tapes, anything you have that you think they'd find helpful. Of course, only include materials that are culturally appropriate for your group. Having something to look at gives people something to do until they know each other a little better.

Acknowledge cultural, racial, and other differences during an early "What do we really want for our kids?" discussion. This is often a good way to form a working alliance among diverse participants and school professionals. You might conclude the discussion by saying, "So, even though we here in this room are different from each other in important ways—ways we can quickly see, such as race or background, and ways we can't see, such as values or religious heritage—we all pretty well agree that we want our kids to . . . "

It is also good to address parents' immediate issues in the first session. What issues brought them to the meeting? What worries them? What is driving them up the wall? Assure parents that their concerns are very important to you and that the group will address them or you'll help them find other places where they can get more help.

Emphasize Active Learning

Once your group is going, remember to encourage liberally! Encourage failings as well as successes—failure means that effort is being expended and progress is being made. Use the example of a sailboat—the way it gets from one side of the lake to the other is by correcting the position of the sail in relation to the wind, over and over. Offer yourself as an example of taking risks to make changes. Have no pretenses: Convey to parents that you aren't a perfect person, but a striving-to-be-better person.

A supportive leader who relates to the participants at their level, engages in two-way conversation, and is willing to listen, encourage, and promote decision making is more likely to make participants feel at ease about becoming involved in the group. Videotape yourself leading the group and view it critically: Is there any part of your posture, tone of voice, gestures, or demeanor that suggests that you wish to dominate, control, or act superior? Sometimes others' perceptions are very different from what we intend, and it is good to get feedback on our performance when we can.

Keep lecturing to a minimum and increase involvement by using games and fun activities. Have large group discussions and small group discussions. Include humor; share favorite cartoons or quips to get things going each week. Use home activities that parents try out and then tell about in the group; reward the parents who venture to "share and tell" with coupons from local merchants.

Start on time and stop on time. This helps respect parents' schedules and your child care volunteers, if you have them.

Aim for Good Closure

Find someone with a computer who can make very attractive certificates for parents who complete the course. Use as many of these thank-you and congratulations rituals as you think your group will enjoy! Helium balloons and a decorated cake are simple touches that communicate a sense of special celebration.

Have parents write an encouraging postcard to themselves (or to each other). Keep the postcards and mail them 30 days after the last meeting.

Ask parents to share their experiences with a friend and encourage them to attend the next session. Remind them that we want all children to have good parenting, both for humanitarian reasons and for selfish reasons. Some counselors have found this sales pitch makes practical sense to parents: "Your child will be going to school with all the children from our community. Poorly parented ones require much more teacher time and detract from a quality education. So help us reach every family you know!"

Take pictures of individual participants and ask them to write down one thing the class has meant to them. Get permission to share these in the future. Ask a local paper to run the pictures and remarks next time you start another program. Ask parents if they'd be willing to give brief testimonials at PTA or other meetings for sponsors or other potential attendees.

Ask parents to fill out evaluations—but keep these simple. Basically, you want to know what worked for them and what didn't. In their view, what would have made the program better? Also ask parents to be specific about changes they've seen in their own lives and their children's lives as a result of the program. If someone later challenges you to show results, can you do it? Only if you ask parents to provide you with this information!

In conclusion, I would like to reiterate that there is no one bridge that will work in connecting with all hard-to-reach parents, but I hope this book has given you a place to begin looking for ideas. Using the support of parents you already know is sure to help you reach out to other parents within the community. Once a relationship is established, remember that it is just as important (though sometimes more difficult—often very rewarding) to maintain that relationship throughout and sometimes beyond the years of a child's education.

Even the most uncommunicative of parents can be reached with enough effort and evidence that you value their opinion. It is crucial, though, that your intentions and determination are clear in your everyday conduct and conversation. As long as you, the counselor, believe that it is essential for you to reach parents and to help them develop skills for parenting—and for life—so that you may provide the best possible environment for children, you will be able to sustain your vision in spite of the many other demands on your time.

Expect parents to reach you and teach you, as well. You will find yourself learning things from them that you didn't know you needed to know! In time, some parents will become trusted partners and allies. They are colleagues worth cultivating. Remember, the support and understanding of parents will augment your ability to foster places in our schools and communities where children can become great.

Resource A:
Resources for Building
Parent Participation

Active Parenting of Teens, Active Parenting for Children Ages 2-12, and
1, 2, 3, 4 *Parents* (video-based parent education), leader training
workshops, *Leader* magazine, and a catalogue of helpful resources
for parents and teachers.

> Active Parenting Publishers
> 810 Franklin Court, Suite B
> Marietta, GA 30067
> 1-800-825-0060

Parents on Board (video-based program for academic support)

Center for Play Therapy
>   Workshops, courses, videotapes, and books on filial therapy.

>   University of North Texas
>   P.O. Box 311337
>   Denton, TX 76203-1337
>   (940) 565-3864 • www.coe.unt.edu\cdhe\cpt

Smart Start for Parents (Send-home video parent education program)

21st Century Learning Institute
>   P.O. Box 515
>   Lopez Island, WA 98261
>   1-800-538-7532

STEP (Systematic Training for Effective Parenting): *STEP, Early Child-hood STEP* and *STEP/Teen* (video-based parent education); leader training workshops, parenting catalog.

>   AGS
>   1-800-328-2560 • www.agsnet.com

The U.S. Government Printing Office sells several documents of interest to those who work with parents and caregivers.

✴ *Grandparents as parents: Raising a second generation.* (Hearing before the Special Committee on Aging, United States Senate, One Hundred Second Congress, second Session, Washington, July 29, 1992.)

Family partnerships: A continuous process. Training guides for the Head Start learning community. (1998). Washington, DC: Department of Health and Human Services, Administration for Children and Families, Administration on Child, Youth, and Families.

✳ *Achieving the goals: Goal 8, Parental involvement and participation.* Department of Education.

Resource B:
Suggested Readings

Atkinson, D. R., & Juntunen C. L. (1994). School counselors and school psychologists as school-home-community liaisons in ethnically diverse schools. In P. Pedersen & J. C. Carey (Eds.), *Multicultural counseling in schools*. Boston: Allyn & Bacon.

Booth, A., & Dunn, J. (Eds.). 1996. *Family-school links: How do they affect educational outcomes?* Mahwah, NJ: Lawrence Erlbaum.

Borodovsky, L. G., & Ponterotto, J. G. (1994). A family-based approach to multicultural career development. In P. Pedersen & J. C. Carey (Eds.), *Multicultural counseling in schools*. Boston: Allyn & Bacon.

Casas, J. M., & Furlong, M. J. (1994). School counselors as advocates for increased Hispanic parent participation in schools. In P. Pedersen & J. C. Carey (Eds.), *Multicultural counseling in schools*. Boston: Allyn & Bacon.

Christenson, S. L. (1995). Families and schools: What is the role of the school psychologist? *School Psychology Quarterly, 10,* 118-132.

Christenson, S. L., Hurley, C. M., Sheridan, S. M., & Fenstermacher, K. (1997). Parents' and school psychologists' perspectives on parent involvement activities. *School Psychology Review, 26,* 111-130.

Cole, S. M., Thomas, A. R., & Lee, C. C. (1988). School counselor and school psychologist: Partners in minority family outreach. *Journal of Multicultural Counseling and Development, 16,* 110-116.

DeToledo, S. (1995). *Grandparents as parents: A survival guide for raising a second family.* New York: Guilford.

Evanoski, P. O., & Tse, F. W. (1989). Career awareness program for Chinese and Korean American parents. *Journal of Counseling and Development, 67,* 472-473.

Gestincki, C. (1996). *Home, school, and community relations* (3rd ed.). Albany, NY: Delmar.

Montgomery, M. J., DeBell, C., & Wilkins, J. (1998). Calming anxiety: Developmental interventions for multigenerational parent-child therapy. *The Family Journal: Counseling and Therapy for Couples and Families, 6*(2), 87-93.

Morrow, R. D. (1989). Southeast-Asian parental involvement: Can it be a reality? *Elementary School Guidance & Counseling, 23,* 289-297.

National PTA. (1997). *National standards for parent/family involvement programs.* Chicago: Author.

Neuman, S. G., Hagedorn, T., Celano, D., & Daly, P. (1995). Toward a collaborative approach to parent involvement in early education: A study of teenage mothers in an African-American community. *American Educational Research Journal, 32,* 801-827.

Perry, C., Williams, C. L., Vebien-Mortenson, S., & Toomey, T. L. (1996). Project Northland: Outcomes of a community-wide alcohol use prevention program during early adolescence. *American Journal of Public Health, 86,* 956-965.

Rupert, H. (1994). The impact of a parent involvement program designed to support a first-grade reading intervention program. In C. K. Kinzer & D. J. Lewu (Eds.), *Multidimensional aspects of literacy research, theory, and practice.* Chicago: National Reading Conference.

Sung, K. W., Kim, J., & Yawkey, T. D. (1997). Puerto Rican parents' understanding of their young children's development: P.I.A.G.E.T. program impacts on family involvement in culturally and linguistically diverse populations. *Psychology in the Schools, 34,* 347-353.

Vopart, J. (1994). *The parent project: A workshop approach to parent involvement.* York, ME: Stenhouse.

References

Brazelton, T. B. (1992). *Touchpoints: Your child's emotional and behavioral development*. Reading, MA: Addison-Wesley.

Erikson, E. (1963). *Childhood and society* (2nd ed.). New York: Norton.

Gottman, J. M., Katz, L. F., & Hooven, C. (1996). Meta-emotion philosophy and the emotional life of families: Theoretical models and preliminary data. *Journal of Family Psychology, 10,* 243-268.

Guerney, L., & Guerney, B. (1989). Child relationship enhancements: Family therapy and parent education. *Person Centered Review, 4,* 344-357.

Kraft, A., & Landreth, G. (1998). Parents as therapeutic partners: Listening to your child's play. Northvale, NJ: Jason Aronson.

Landreth, G. (1991). Play therapy: The art of the relationship. Muncie, IN: Accelerated Development Press.

Maslow, A. H. (1970). *Motivation and personality* (2nd ed.). Princeton, NJ: Van Nostrand.

Parents on Board. (Video). (1995). Marietta, GA: Active Parenting Publishers.

Popkin, M. (1987). *Archive Parenting: Teaching cooperation, courage, and responsibility.* San Francisco: HarperCollins.

Popkin, M. H., Gard, B., & Montgomery, M. (1996). *Parents workbook: Parenting your 1- to 4-year old.* Atlanta, GA: Active Parenting Publishers.

Sklare, G. B. (1997). *Brief counseling that works: A solution-focused approach for school counselors.* Thousand Oaks, CA: Corwin.

Smart Start for Parents. (Video). (1994). 21st Century Learning Institute, P.O. Box 515, Lopez Island, WA 98261.

Index

Active Parenting workshops, 54, 55, 67, 77
Anxiety in parents:
  benefits of, 33
  hazards of, 33-34
  reducing, 38-44
  See also Good-enough parent;
    Overindulgence of children

Bridges to parents:
  gaining cooperation for, 24-27
  deciding goal of, 17
  maintaining, 28-31. *See also*
    Conferences with parents
  removing obstacles for, 19

Career genograms, 53-54
Child-environment fit, 42
Conferences with parents, 29-31
  Conflict with parents, 71
  planning guide for, 30 (figure)

Cultural differences, 19-21, 37, 44, 73-74
  and obstacles to career
    exploration, 53 (figure)
  and student vocational success,
    52-53, 54 (figure)
  See also Trust, creating

Development:
  of parents as adults, 5-9
  of normal children, 38-39

Emotion coaching, 58-59, 60-63
  (figure)
Erikson, E., 7

Filial therapy, 55-58

Good-enough parent, 39. *See also*
  Anxiety in parents
Grandparents raising children, 44-45, 78

Home visits, 6, 15

Landreth, G., 55

Narrative therapy, 34

Orientations to parent
    involvement:
    developmental, 47
    process orientation to, 47
    task orientation to, 46-47
    See also Parent empowerment;
        Parenting programs
Overindulgence of children, 34-35.
    See also Anxiety in parents

Parent empowerment, 11-13, 51,
    59, 63-65. *See also* Parenting
    programs
Parent involvement:
    benefits to children, 3-4
    guidelines for, 48 (figure)
    opportunities for, 49-51
    reluctance about, 22-23
Parenting programs, 54, 55, 77-78
    planning, 67-70
    implementing, 70-75
    first meetings of, 73-74
Parents:
    competence of, 10

effectiveness of, 4
enmeshment of, 35-36
needs of, 6, 67
self-efficacy of, 9, 35. *See also*
    Parent empowerment
Parent's Affirmation of Imperfection,
    41
Parents on Board, 52, 77, 81
Perfectionism, 39-42
Problem Solving
Popkin, M., 40, 41, 81

Research, counselor's use of, 43
Respect:
    for parents, 11, 13
School counselor:
    demands on, 1-2
    role of, 1-2
    genuineness of, 23-24

Smart Start for Parents, 52, 77, 82
Social support, 4-5
Student academic success
    promoting, 51-52
Systems perspective, 39

Trust, 8
    creating, 14-16, 20, 23
    See also Cultural differences